1·95

PIANO

PIANO
Trevor Griffiths

A new play for theatre

based on the film

Unfinished Piece

for Mechanical Piano

by A. Adabashyan and

N. Mikhalkov

ff

faber and faber

LONDON · BOSTON

First published in 1990
by Faber and Faber Limited
3 Queen Square London WC1N 3AU

Photoset by Parker Typesetting Service Leicester
Printed in Great Britain by Clays Ltd St Ives plc

© Trevor Griffiths, 1990

Trevor Griffiths is hereby identified as author of this work in accordance with
Section 77 of the Copyright, Designs and Patents Act 1988.

All professional and amateur rights are strictly reserved and applications to
perform them must be made in advance to A. D. Peters and Co. Ltd, 5th Floor,
The Chambers, Chelsea Harbour, Lots Road, London SW10 OXF.

*This book is sold subject to the condition that it shall not, by way of trade or otherwise,
be lent, resold, hired out or otherwise circulated without the publisher's prior consent in
any form of binding or cover other than that in which it is published and without a
similar condition including this condition being imposed on the subsequent purchaser.*

A CIP record for this book is available from
the British Library

ISBN 0-571-16176-6

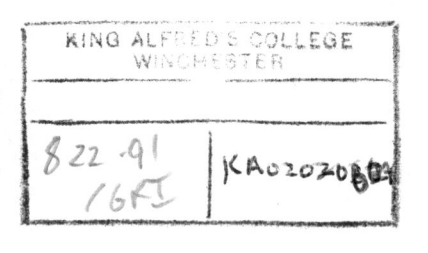

AUTHOR'S PREFACE

The text that follows is a theatrical mediation of Adabashyan and
Mikhalkov's remarkable *Unfinished Piece for Mechanical Piano*
(1980), itself an imaginative filmic reworking of themes from
Chekhov's plays (most notably *Platonov*) and his short fiction.
The Russian film-makers, whether out of respect or simple
unconcern, have allowed me to plunder their own piece in order
to find my own; and I'm truly grateful for the generous space
they've afforded me.

If I call *Piano* a new play, then, it is in part because I have no
right to saddle them (or indeed Chekhov) with the piece I've
finally fashioned. For while in respect of character, relationship,
incident and dramatic terrain, *Piano* draws heavily on these
several ur-works, there is yet within it, at the level of tone,
language, form, means and intentions, something other than what
they have sought to say, for which I must both claim and accept
full responsibility.

As to what exactly that something other is and where precisely
it might be found upon the tragicomic map of the human project,
I can at this stage, a month ahead of the play's first rehearsal,
usefully say nothing. So let me instead offer a context for a
possible reading of the piece with a passage from the late and
deeply missed Raymond Williams:

The condition of realism in the nineteenth century was in fact an
assumption of a total world. In the great realists, there was no separation
in kind between public and private facts, or between public and private
experience. This was not, as it may easily appear in retrospect, a wilful
joining of disparate things. Rather, it was a way of seeing the world in
which it was possible to experience the quality of a whole way of life
through the qualities of individual men and women. Thus, a personal
breakdown was a genuinely social fact, and a social breakdown was lived
and known in direct personal experience . . . Chekhov is the realist of
breakdown, on a significantly total scale.

Modern Tragedy, 1966

Should *Piano* prove to be about anything at all, I suspect it may prove, like its illustrious forebears, to be about just this felt sense of breakdown and deadlock; and thus perhaps, in a nicely perverse irony, about what it's like to be living in our own post-capitalist, post-socialist, post-realist, post-modern times.

Trevor Griffiths
Boston Spa
24 May 1990

Piano was first performed at the Cottesloe Theatre, London, on 8 August 1990. The cast was as follows:

RADISH	Keith Bartlett
ZAKHAR	Kevin O'Donohoe
TRILETSKI	Oliver Cotton
ANNA	Penelope Wilton
PORFIRY	Geoffrey Palmer
SERGEI	Duncan Bell
YASHA	Peter Caffrey
PETRIN	Stephen Moore
PLATONOV	Stephen Rea
SASHENKA	Julia Ford
COLONEL	Basil Henson
SOPHIA	Suzanne Burden
SHCHERBUK	Philip Voss
PETYA	Robbie Engels
GOROKHOV	Michael O'Connor

Director	Howard Davies
Designer	Ashley Martin-Davis
Lighting	Chris Parry
Music	Dominic Muldowney
Dance	Jane Gibson

A southern province of Russia in the early summer of 1904. The garden, terrace and veranda of the late General Voynitsev's estate.

ACT ONE

Black.

RADISH: (*From above, unseen*) It's all right, little peasant. We can do it, we can get it over. Everything's possible.
(*Bring up shadowy unreal light. Two men hump a large, heavy object wrapped in cowhide across a high narrow plank bridge. The work is hard, precarious; the men sweat, strain, their progress bruisingly slow.* RADISH, *the older of the two, gaunt and cropped, guides the younger.*)
Left. Straight. Easy.
(*They inch precariously out on to the planks.*)
(*Eventually*) Rest, Zakhar.
(*The load's lowered.* ZAKHAR, *young and dreamy, sucks for air.* RADISH *edges round the load to test the planking ahead.* ZAKHAR *slumps to a sit, stares down into the drop below.*)

ZAKHAR: Let's find another way, Radish. It's too risky, this. Radish?

RADISH: (*Mind on problem*) There is no other way. If there's another way, what are we doing here?
(*He walks carefully back to the load, studies its shape and outline, scrutinizes the labels stuck on to the hide.*)

ZAKHAR: What is it? Does it say?

RADISH: (*Face to wrapping*) This? Cowhide. (*He looks at the youth, grins weirdly.*) Says it's a machine. Come from Moscow. Two thousand roubles.
(*Silence.* ZAKHAR *deals with the unimaginable.*)

ZAKHAR: Don't, Radish. You're tickling me again.

RADISH: (*Finger to label*) Two thousand roubles. See for yourself.

ZAKHAR: Is it possible?
(RADISH *chuckles, an odd growling sound. Sits to rest.*)

RADISH: Anything's possible.

ZAKHAR: (*Serious; after thought*) Zzish. No wonder it's so heavy.
(*They sit in silence, staring out. Bleed in birdsong, breeze in*

trees, running water below; the sound is hollow, alienated, as unreal as the light.)

My Aunt Katya says if you look up at the heavens without blinking you can see the angels.

(*Silence.* ZAKHAR *stares upwards.*)

Tiny little angels on high, flapping their wings and going zzihzzih like mosquitoes. Read me some more of your story, eh?

RADISH: What for? You've heard it a hundred times.

ZAKHAR: It's a fine tale.

RADISH: It's not a tale. It's my life. (*He takes out a grubby notebook from his pocket, thumbs pages.*) Where was I?

ZAKHAR: Moscow.

RADISH: (*Eventually*) 'Moscow. Everything seemed possible. He had found work as a house painter, learned roofing and glazing, and landed a contract to work on the building of a new railway station in the suburbs. Twelve men he paid from his own pocket, a peasant from Zukhovo, son of serfs.' (*Long silence.*) 'The second winter it rained fifty-nine days in a row. The men were laid off, he made do with odd jobs in the city, painting, papering walls. But rain or shine, the police were round to his lodgings every week for their bribe money. The last job he took was in a gentlemen's club, papering the reading room. He'd agreed seven kopeks a roll with the committee, but when he came to get paid the steward told him to sign for twelve. Perhaps he had a cold or a toothache, it wasn't the first time he had been asked to fiddle an employer's books, but he refused. The steward called the chairman, a handsome, cultured gentleman with gold-rimmed spectacles, who listened carefully to the steward's account, then handed our hero the pen and said: "One more word from you, you miserable bag of snot, and I'll smash your face in."'

(*Silence.* ZAKHAR *gives him a look.*)

ZAKHAR: What did he do?

RADISH: (*Resuming*) 'He said "With respect, sir . . ."' And the gentleman smashed his face in. Next day the police took him in, the gents club had charged him with fraud and extortion.

When the case came to court, the very policeman he'd been paying bribe money to for a year and more testified he had left his village of Zukhovo without a permit and that was that. Four years in Siberia. Penal settlement.'

(*Silence.* RADISH *strokes his cropped head.* ZAKHAR *watches.*)

ZAKHAR: Sometimes, Radish, I think the Lord does not like the peasant.

(RADISH *looks at the blond dreamy youth a moment, pockets his book, smiles.*)

RADISH: It's possible, Zakhar.

ZAKHAR: That's where you met the General, mm?

RADISH: Mm. Among others. So many strange folk there. Some who would eat only vegetables, mm?

(ZAKHAR *shakes his head, bewildered.*)

Some who believed the Lord God would come again amongst us to bring down the corrupt and the powerful. Still others who believed it was the peasants themselves who would rise up and smite the oppressor.

(ZAKHAR *purses his lips, shakes his head.*)

I learned reading there. And writing. And thinking.

ZAKHAR: All men think, Radish.

RADISH: All men have thoughts, maybe. Thinking's different. Thinking has to be learned. Like making bombs. And laying them.

(*Silence. A voice calls from the distance:* Zakhar. Zakhar. Zakhar. *The men ignore it.*)

ZAKHAR: You learned those things there?

(RADISH *nods.* ZAKHAR *shakes his head. The call again.* RADISH *levers himself upright, begins imaging the journey across the planks.*)

RADISH: Yasha.

ZAKHAR: Yasha.

(RADISH *tests the planks again with his foot.* ZAKHAR *takes out a small mouth organ, begins a low, haunting melody.* RADISH *listens a moment, a smile on his lips.*)

RADISH: Will we go?

ZAKHAR: Tell me about the bird.

RADISH: Again?

(ZAKHAR *grins.*)
And *then* we go?
(ZAKHAR *nods, swivels to watch him out on the planks.*)
All right. About a year into my sentence, I was detailed to restore the icons in the Regimental Chapel. When the General saw what I could do, he put me to work at the big house on his wife's holy pictures. His first wife, yes? Not this . . . pretty one. She was sick, well she was dying, there was nothing he would not do to ease her going . . . He even came home one day with a big green parrot, for company while he was away. Some days before she left this world, she asked to see her dearest icons. I'd been working flat out on them for months to have them ready. I took them into her chamber and held them up in turn for her. Our Lady of Khazan. Our Lady of Smolensk. Our Lady of the Three Arms. Her eyes filled with tears when she saw them. She muttered something, I stooped to catch her words. (*Dark, hoarse, unreal voice*) 'Do me one last kindness, my man, that I might go to my grave in peace.'
(*His hand stretches out across the room he's back in.* ZAKHAR *stares slack-mouthed, deep in the performance.*)
'Kill that bloody parrot. I cannot get a wink of sleep for it.'
(ZAKHAR *laughs, claps his hands.* RADISH *bows ironically.*)
ZAKHAR: Is there anything at all you believe in, Radish?
RADISH: Believe in, maybe not. But there are things I know.
ZAKHAR: What things?
RADISH: Grass dies. Iron rusts. Lies eat the soul. Everything's possible.
(*The voice calls* ZAKHAR *again.* RADISH *takes his place at the rear of the load,* ZAKHAR *at the front. They suck air, dip, lift, totter forward.*)

Slow crossfade to:
YASHA, *in butler's tails and tie, trying to disengage a lady's corset from the branch of a garden tree with a long pole. He calls from time to time:* Zakhar. Zakhar. Zakhar. *Curses. Resumes his task. Voices, laughter from behind him.*
Fade up:

4

A samovar, steaming gently. Near by, TRILETSKI *and* ANNA *play chess at a garden table.* PETRIN *sits in a deckchair some distance away, his back to them, reading a newspaper. Further off, a slung hammock, empty.*

TRILETSKI: (*Off laughter*) . . . It's true. Right there in the orangery.
    (ANNA *looks up, smiles faintly, returns to the game, cigarette in mouth.*)
    Then there was the case of the Kalitins' daughter . . . remember the Kalitins? Kalusha?
    (ANNA *nods vaguely.*)
    Built like a goose. Of course, I was a younger man then, and still a touch shy. What a time I had with their Kalusha, I was never off the premises, her father had to take out a bank loan to pay for the coffee I drank . . .
ANNA: Sh. You stop me thinking.
TRILETSKI: (*A look, a move*) Check.
    (*He carries his cup to the samovar, shortens a little to check teeth and hair in the steel reflection.*)
    Well, I was staying over one weekend, it's two in the morning, I'm all tucked up in my little monk's bed there when . . . click . . . the door opens . . .
    (*He looks across at* ANNA; *is pleased to have her attention*)
    and . . . my heart was pounding like a cannon, you can imagine . . .
ANNA: I can imagine. Get to the point.
TRILETSKI: It's too humiliating.
ANNA: An illicit visit from your little goose? How?
TRILETSKI: (*Refilling cup*) It wasn't her. It was the old maidservant, eighty at least, deaf as a bell, with an enema bottle in her hand, mm? And, if you'll pardon the indelicacy, insisting on giving me one.
    (ANNA *laughs. He returns to the table, pleased.*)
    I raised no objection. I never argue with the deaf. In any case, I thought it might be a custom in the house. Next day it turned out she'd come into the wrong room. But it put an end to the romance, I'll tell you . . . Funny, eh?
ANNA: (*Laughing*) No. Vulgar. Here.

5

(*She holds a cigarette out for him. He leans forward to take it in his lips. Sounds of people approaching off.*)

TRILETSKI: Merci, mon ange.

ANNA: Pas du tout.

TRILETSKI: Je brûle pour une cigarette.

ANNA: Ah oui?

(*She gives him a dark, smouldery look. He takes it for a moment, at length is happy to escape to the safety of the approaching voices.* YASHA, *pole still up, stops mid-probe to check arrivals.*)

PORFIRY: (*Off*) Like that. Hunh? Like that. D'ye see? Like that.

(PORFIRY – *shy, gentle, late fifties; a landowner – enters, in full calling gear save a coat, scythe in his hands, demonstrating a mowing movement on the still air for someone behind him not yet visible. He turns, as* SERGEI, *small dog under one arm, Porfiry's jacket over the other, shepherds on a young* PEASANT, *the object of the exercise.*)

You understand?

(*He demonstrates the movement again. The* PEASANT *nods sourly, cap in hand.*)

Here, take it.

(*The young* PEASANT *takes the scythe.* SERGEI – *thirty; in fine linen peasant smock – waves him away.*)

SERGEI: . . . Nevertheless, Porfiry Semyonovich, it is in such pure and simple-hearted peasants that our country's moral strength resides.

(*He hands* PORFIRY *his jacket, helps him with it.*)

PORFIRY: Perhaps it is, perhaps it isn't, dear Sergei, but where will any of us be if they can't use a scythe properly? In my day, we held quite different beliefs. Our moral strength was based on chivalry. It was woman *we* worshipped. We put her on a different plane, as the better being, the salvation of the species. (*Looks shyly across at* ANNA.) And so she is still.

ANNA: How did this pawn get here?

TRILETSKI: (*Glancing at board*) Which?

ANNA: This one. Who put it there?

TRILETSKI: You did.

ANNA: Ridiculous.

TRILETSKI: You did. Are you suggesting . . . ?

ANNA: Oh yes. (*Laughs.*) Pardon, monsieur.
> (*They laugh, close, intimate.* PORFIRY *turns away, heads for the* samovar, SERGEI *in tow.*)

PORFIRY: In my day, one went through fire for one's loved ones. Nowadays . . .

SERGEI: . . . Nowadays we have the fire brigade. (*He laughs* brayingly at his joke. PORFIRY *sniffs, debating tea.* ANNA *and* TRILETSKI *exchange a dry look.*)
> Jokes on one side, I must pursue my theme. The common folk are, in the view of many of us, as rain clouds hovering over the fields of humanity, in which the seeds of our future are already sown and waiting . . .
> (ANNA *begins to whistle 'The Marseillaise' very badly.* SERGEI *bobs closer to* PORFIRY.)
> Mama doesn't like this kind of talk, of course. Poor Russia. Come on, Voltaire.
> (*He lays the dog down, walks away towards the hammock,* clicking his fingers. The dog watches him. SERGEI *stops,* remonstrates in dumb show, fingers clicking. The dog looks away, uninterested.)

TRILETSKI: You are an amazing woman.
> (ANNA *stops whistling, looks up at him inquiringly.*)
> You whistle just like a navvy. Your move.

ANNA: I'm bored.
> (*She looks at* PORFIRY, *who bows, eager to serve; smiles; looks* at PETRIN, head in paper.)
> Read me something, Gerasim.
> (PETRIN *grunts.*)
> Something romantic.

TRILETSKI: It's quite a different matter when she's winning. 'I'm bored' means 'I'm losing'. If we don't continue, I shall assume you concede.

ANNA: Assume what you will.

TRILETSKI: (*Totting up*) Very well, that's . . . ten roubles you owe me . . .

ANNA: (*A whipcrack*) Yasha!
> (YASHA's *at full stretch, corsets all but accomplished; the call rips* him off balance, the pole swirls dangerously around.)

7

YASHA: (*Icy*) Could it wait, madame?

ANNA: Is there any sign of Zakhar and that other one? And what about the gypsies? Finish that at once and come and speak to me . . .

(*She looks across at* TRILETSKI, *who's emptied a biscuit bag and is now quietly inflating it; follows his eyes to* SERGEI, *who's down on all fours some paces from the impassive mutt, mid-lecture.* TRILETSKI *holds the bag out very deliberately, bursts it with a bang of the hand.* SERGEI *yelps, rears.*)

SERGEI: Maman, tell him. I do despise that sort of thing . . .

(ANNA *chuckles.* SERGEI *moves off for the hammock.*)

TRILETSKI: What about your debt? How will you pay me?

(*A moment. She gives him another smoulder. He braves it out. She blows smoke in his face.*)

ANNA: (*Rising*) Sergei, pay this clown ten roubles.

SERGEI: (*Sulking*) . . . No, Maman, no . . . When father was alive . . . I don't know . . . (*He slumps into the hammock.*) Even Voltaire doesn't love me . . .

(YASHA *approaches, the pole held like a lance, the corsets on the tip. He walks deliberately, headed for the house.*)

YASHA: (*On the move, eyes front*) A telegram has been despatched to the gypsies. Zakhar and the other one left for the station first thing and are expected imminently . . .

ANNA: Where did you find that?

YASHA: (*On and gone*) In a tree, madame.

(TRILETSKI *chuckles.* PETRIN *stares at the corset from behind his paper.* PORFIRY, *on the edge of things, looks away, embarrassed.*)

TRILETSKI: (*On his feet; posing a little*) I think. I shall drink. A little wine.

(*He saunters off for the house. Passes the sitting dog, clicks his fingers without looking back. The mutt wags after him on cue.*)

SERGEI: Look at him. Look at him.

(ANNA *stands for a moment, fixes eventually on* PORFIRY; *smiles.* PORFIRY *gives her his rictal bow.*)

ANNA: So, Porfiry Semyonovich.

(*He waits, expectant.*)

Won't you join me?

(*He approaches the table, she indicates Triletski's chair, he sits, she joins him across the table, carefully removes the buffering chessboard.*)

Woman is the better human being, did you say?

PORFIRY: (*A touch breathless*) Better. Most certainly. Oh yes.

ANNA: (*Low, intimate*) And you're a great lover . . . of women, is that right?

PORFIRY: I most certainly do . . . love them. Adore them. Yes.

ANNA: (*The tease on*) Them? How many have you known?

PORFIRY: Women?

ANNA: Mm.

PORFIRY: Believe me, Anna Petrovna, if I had known only one . . . and that one were you . . . it would suffice.

(*Long pause, as she holds him in her gaze. He trembles.*)

ANNA: (*Soft, wicked*) Boobooboobooboo . . .

(PORFIRY *blinks. Giggles.* ANNA *laughs. A loud flatulent blast draws attention to the house, where* TRILETSKI *has reappeared on a first-floor balcony with wine, telescope and a hunting horn.*)

TRILETSKI: God be praised. Here come the Platonovs. At last!

SERGEI: Hurrah. Hurrah. Hurrah.

ANNA: Good. (*She looks at the three men about her.*) And what do we think of Platonov?

(*Silence.*)

PORFIRY: I lost a cufflink when I was mowing . . . Mikhail? He's a clever enough fellow . . . I'd better see if I can find it . . .

(*He wanders away.* PETRIN *stands, folds his paper carefully, pockets his glasses. He's in his forties, neat, strong, meticulous.*)

SERGEI: Misha's a man among men. A delight to converse with.

(ANNA *cues* PETRIN *to give voice.*)

PETRIN: Talks well. Lacks sense.

TRILETSKI: (*Telescope up*) Ha ha. He's blown up like a bull, my little sister's risen like a bunloaf. They must have spent the whole winter at the trough.

(ANNA *rises to greet the newcomers.* PLATONOV *arrives, mopping his face and drying the band of his panama, his wife* SASHENKA *some steps behind. She wears a pretty new flower-braided hat, a slender but worrying fraction too large for her head.*)

ANNA: Welcome. At last. Would you care for tea?

PLATONOV: Tea? No.

(*He sits heavily.* SERGEI *greets* SASHENKA *with a deep bow and a handkiss.*)

Well, I see there are still people in the world. We haven't encountered a soul for six months. Winters are God's greatest mistake. How are you then, madame? Still making your stepson miserable?

ANNA: Not at all. He's even started calling me Mama.

PLATONOV: Eat, sleep, talk to the walls . . . Dreary.

SASHENKA: (*Joining them at table*) Dreary? Why so, Misha? A little dull, perhaps, but pleasant enough, surely?

(*She adjusts the brim of her hat, smiling, lovely and nervous.* PLATONOV *stares at her in minatory silence for a moment, looks away. Nods greeting to* PETRIN. *Glimpses* PORFIRY *on the fringe, stooped in search of his cufflink.*)

ANNA: Well, you're both looking remarkably . . . sleek. It must be a measure of how happy you are together . . .

(PLATONOV *glares at her a moment; leaves his seat.*)

PLATONOV: That you, Porfiry Semyonovich? You can't hide from me, I see everything.

(PORFIRY *stands briefly, bows. Shows his shirt sleeve.*)

PORFIRY: Cuff. Lost it. Link.

(*He disappears again.*)

PLATONOV: (*Peering myopically*) Sergei? Is it you? Where's the long hair and choirboy voice?

SERGEI: All gone, Misha. I'm a bass now.

PLATONOV: A bass, eh? Mm.

(ANNA *and* SASHENKA *laugh.* PLATONOV *grins.*)

Well, what does your stepmother have in store for us, mm?

ANNA: There are gypsies coming, God willing. And there's a small musical surprise on its way.

(*Thunder, remote, rolling in.*)

PLATONOV: Good. I like a surprise.

(*Silence.*)

ANNA: I believe it might rain.

(PETRIN *moves to another chair closer to the house, resumes his tour of the paper.* PLATONOV *stands immobile, as if weighed down.* SASHENKA *approaches him, giggles something in his ear.*)

PLATONOV: Sergei, Sergei, Sergei my dear fellow, got yourself wed and never said a word.

(SERGEI *approaches shyly, pleased, takes the congratulating hand.*)

SERGEI: A whirlwind, dear friend. Blew me head over heels. Whoo.

SASHENKA: (*Kissing his cheek*) Bless you, bless you. Now you will discover life's deepest joys . . .

PLATONOV: . . . You'll excuse my wife. Weddings make her heady. (*Some laughter.* SASHENKA *rebalances her hat.*)

SASHENKA: It's not weddings, Misha. It's order. You've made me very happy, Sergei Pavlovich.

SERGEI: (*Hugging and lifting her*) Me too, Sashenka. I've never ever been so happy, never ever . . .

(PLATONOV *leaves them to their celebration. Stares at* ANNA *darkly. She begins to chuckle.*)

PLATONOV: What?

ANNA: (*Chuckling on*) What?

PLATONOV: What's funny?

(ANNA *turns away, hand to mouth. The separate moments die away. People stand on, smiling or not. Silence grows.*)

PETRIN: (*From nowhere*) It says here a crow was caught by a girl last week in Syzran with blue eyes.

(*Pause.*)

PLATONOV: (*Quiet, deadly*) Good old Syzran. Home of the blue-eyed crow.

ANNA: Porfiry, be so kind as to go and fetch Sophia. I believe she's on the pond.

(PORFIRY *stands, bows, leaves. Thunder again, a touch closer.*)

SERGEI: Ah yes, thoughtless of me, I er . . . I hope nobody imagines I'm like some Arab sheikh who keeps his wives under lock and key . . .

(*He laughs nervously;* SASHENKA *giggles;* PLATONOV *looks at his feet: it's clear no one does.*)

. . . In any case, my beautiful wife is not at all the sort of woman . . .

(*A shot bangs out, loud, sudden, very close. The group leaps to life.*)

TRILETSKI: (*On balcony, hunting rifle in one hand, red wine in the other; calling*) Long live my relatives! All hail to the General's delicious widow!

(*Laughter, calls of reproach.* YASHA *comes out on to the veranda terrace to check on the latest madness; throws himself face down to the ground as* TRILETSKI *looses off another round directly above.* PLATONOV *has brightened; for the first time smiles.*)

PLATONOV: (*Calling*) All hail to the General's delicious widow's impoverished personal physician!

(*The* COLONEL *wobbles out, a gaunt ancient with a knitted shawl round his shoulders and a birch broom at the port in his bony mitts.*)

COLONEL: What? What?

YASHA: (*Recovering slowly*) Your son, Colonel. Having his fun.

PLATONOV: (*Advancing to house, wiping head with kerchief*) . . . God, I can smell it from here, man, you must have been at it all day . . .

TRILETSKI: (*Bottle aloft*) Hail Jupiter, God and Bull! I shall bring you a glass . . .

COLONEL: (*To approaching* PLATONOV) Misha, is it? Who's he firing at?

PLATONOV: Me. Who else would he fire at?

COLONEL: Why?

PLATONOV: You never taught him to shake hands, Colonel.

COLONEL: Did he hit you?

(PLATONOV *ponders the question. The others have followed up the garden; the old man sees his daughter.*)

(*Excited*) Aha, the most beautiful planet in the Triletski firmament.

(*Warm embraces:* SASHENKA, PLATONOV.)

Come and sit down. (*To* PLATONOV) Sit, that's an order. Are you well, my lovely? I'm always well, heart's been a problem now and again, but that's the fair sex and quite incurable . . . Where'd this broom come from? How's my grandson . . . ?

SASHENKA: Blooming. He sends his love.

COLONEL: Sends his love, eh? Bright baby . . .

SERGEI: Metaphorically speaking, she means.

(ANNA *arrives last, lighting another cigarette.*)

COLONEL: . . . Anna Petrovna, my dear lady, I've bought myself . . .

(YASHA *walks past him, removes broom from his hands en route.*) . . . What are *you* doing? . . . I've bought a new shotgun, we'll hunt quail together . . . Oh, look at her, I love 'em like that, there's female liberation for you, kiss her shoulder, she smells of gunpowder . . . Goddess Diana, Alexandra the Great, your Excellency.

PLATONOV: You've been at the bottle too, Colonel, when did you start?

COLONEL: (*Cackling*) Crack o' dawn. Sans doute. House was asleep when I got here, stamped my feet and lo! out she comes, Diana herself, with a laugh and a bottle of Madeira, she had a couple of glasses and I had the rest. Ha!

ANNA: (*Mock angry*) Tell the world, Colonel, won't you.

COLONEL: Aiee. I'm worn out.

(SASHENKA *helps him to a chair.* TRILETSKI *appears from the house, glasses, bottle, telescope in hands.*)

TRILETSKI: Eh bien. Me voici.

(*Laughter, greetings.* SASHENKA *claps her hands. He lays down his load.*)

There you are, my little sister.

(*They embrace.*)

What's this? A new hat! Looks good enough to eat.

(*He plays kid's teasing games with her, affectionate and patronizing, as he prepares his approach to* PLATONOV.)

Oh, and who's this? Not his Excellency!

(PLATONOV *grins, stands. They approach each other in silence, look as if they might fight, segue into customary and personal greeting rituals. Eventually:*)

Comment ça va, Michel?

PLATONOV: (*Slow*) That's a long and very dreary story, Kolya.

(*The group has settled around them.* PETRIN *is back to his paper; the* COLONEL *heads back to sleep;* SASHENKA *watches brother and husband, a nervous smile on her face;* ANNA *sits in a kind of quiet disinterested vacancy;* SERGEI *stares down the garden, on the look-out for his wife.* TRILETSKI *takes a false nose/ moustache mask from his pocket, looks across at the preoccupied*

SERGEI. PLATONOV *follows the look, a smile's shared,* TRILETSKI *dons the mask, the two men join hands and waltz gently around the terrace, humming their music for tempo. Arrive eventually behind* SERGEI.)

TRILETSKI: (*Sudden; weird voice*) . . . Excuse me, my man, I wonder if you could . . .
    (SERGEI *turns sharply, yelps at the mad face. Laughter.*)

SERGEI: (*Moving to other side of terrace*) Nikolai Ivanovich, I do not care for your japes. Tell him, Maman . . .
    (*He whitters on. The laughter seeps away. People settle in the space. The* COLONEL *snores thinly.* SASHENKA *giggles, embarrassed. Silence.*)

TRILETSKI: How's the boy, is he well?

PLATONOV: He's well.

TRILETSKI: Haven't seen him for . . . months and months. He must have grown.

PLATONOV: He's grown.

TRILETSKI: Tall, eh?

PLATONOV: Ahunh.

TRILETSKI: What, really tall? Tall-tall?

PLATONOV: Perhaps. We'll know better when he can stand . . .
    (SASHENKA *chuckles along with the exchange from her chair by the house wall; watches others closely, to be sure things are well. The* COLONEL *farts in his sleep: a slow tearing crack.*)

TRILETSKI: Oh dear!

SASHENKA: (*Crossing*) Papa, please, Papa . . .

COLONEL: I'm awake, I'm awake . . .

SASHENKA: Don't sleep here, I beg you, Papa . . .
    (*She fusses over him, can't shift him.*)

COLONEL: It's your brother's fault, he makes them put beans in the cabbage soup, last week he put salt in my tobacco and sewed up all my pockets . . .
    (PLATONOV *laughs,* TRILETSKI *chuckles,* SASHENKA *shushes the old man quiet.* SERGEI *has collected the telescope; gazes down the garden through it.*)

SERGEI: And here she comes! My beloved wife, Sophia Yegorovna . . .
    (PLATONOV *cuts mid-laugh at the name.* SERGEI *lifts his voice.*)

. . . I thought you had stolen her from me, Porfiry
Semyonovich . . .
(*People drift to the front of the terrace to greet her.* PLATONOV
takes the telescope; refocuses; gazes at the approaching figures.)

SASHENKA: Oh, doesn't she look lovely!
(PLATONOV *lays down the telescope, hovers uneasily, leaves for
the house. Only* ANNA *notes the departure.*)

SOPHIA: (*On the approach, flowers in her hand*) It's wonderful here.
The good Porfiry showed me everything . . .

PORFIRY: (*Toiling after her*) Wait till you see my place. She's
promised you'll come over on Thursday, Sergei . . .
(PLATONOV *appears by a window, pours a drink, swigs it down,
takes another, disappears.*)

SERGEI: . . . Thursday's fine. Perhaps we could all go,
Maman . . .

ANNA: So long as we don't have to call on Yuspov on the way . . .

PLATONOV: (*Reappeared; quietly*) . . . We could go via Platonov's
little plot . . .

PORFIRY: . . . That's miles out of the way . . .

SOPHIA: . . . Platonov's? You know, I believe I knew him once,
Misha Platonov, I don't suppose he's Misha any longer . . .
Mikhail . . . what was it . . . ?

PLATONOV: . . . Vasilyevich . . .

SOPHIA: Vasilyevich. (*She nods her thanks to the stranger, returns to
her flowers.*) Exactly.
(*Silence. Looks exchanged, glances at the still, amiable*
PLATONOV: *something's on.*)

SERGEI: Cher Michel! Never stirs himself but nothing escapes
him . . . (*To* SOPHIA) It's the man in question, my love . . .
See.
(*She turns, stares at* PLATONOV.)

SOPHIA: No. It can't be.
(*Laughter, a touch nervy.*)

PLATONOV: (*Sweet still*) Well, what is it, seven years? Eight? A
long time, Sophia Yegorovna. If we were dogs, we'd already
be geriatric. Horses too.

PETRIN: (*Over paper*) Horses live to eighteen. That's an average,
you understand.

(*Laughter, some relief.*)

SOPHIA: Mikhail Vasilyevich is quite right, it was a long time ago
... another age. He was a student then, I was going to be an
actress, remember? Great things were expected of him,
people said he'd be a future Minister of State. Or a second
Lord Byron, mm? A long time ago. A long way away. How
are you? What are you doing?

PLATONOV: I'm a teacher. Local school.

SOPHIA: No. You?

PLATONOV: Yes. Me.

SOPHIA: I just can't ... Why?

PLATONOV: Why? Because.

SOPHIA: I'm sorry, what I mean is, with a whole world out there
... and a degree ...

PLATONOV: No degree. I gave up.

(*Silence. She frowns, mire ahead of her.*)

SOPHIA: Yes, but that hasn't prevented you becoming a fully
realized ... person, being, human being, has it?

PLATONOV: Excuse me? I'm not sure I've understood your
question ... What?

SOPHIA: Forgive me, I put it badly ...

(*She looks to* SERGEI *for help, he smiles supportively: he's
having a bad time.*)

I mean: none of this stops you from wanting to create a better
world, reform, progress, the rights of women, that kind of
thing, does it? You can still serve ideals, can't you ... ?

PLATONOV: ... But of course, Sophia Yegorovna. Do not for a
moment imagine we have let ourselves go here. I can assure
you we are as abreast and as busy as any in the land,
appearances notwithstanding ... Triletski here, a simple
district doctor you might think, but no, a *Darwinist*, mm, an
evolutionist even, a man moreover who has dedicated much
of his time – some might even say a disproportionate amount
of it – to the Woman Question ... Porfiry Semyonovich,
landowner, yes, but so much more – an authority on grass-
mowing techniques. And popular hygiene. Shaves his
peasants' skulls every week, a whole village, you'll see for
yourself, they look like actors. We take all the major

newspapers and journals, Petrin there kindly collates them and reads them out to us . . . (*He picks up Sashenka's straw hat, puts it on his head.*) So you see, dear lady, we certainly do our share of toiling here . . . Ah yes, I quite forgot, my wife . . . (*He gathers her by the arm, draws her forward.*) . . . my wife Alexandra, Sashenka, Sashenka, my wife, civic responsibility, reproduction of the species, we've been busy multiplying, I have a son on whom to bequeath my ideas. No actual wealth, of course, but what's that compared with intellectual inheritance . . .

(*He sits, still wearing Sashenka's hat, as if drained by the passage from irony to mania.* SOPHIA *finds it difficult to look anywhere.* ANNA *sits detached, ironically watchful; whistles a snatch of 'Una Furtiva Lacrima'. Silence.* YASHA *enters suddenly with a tray of drinks,* TRILETSKI *turns him around and heads him back off. A train whistles in the distance.* SOPHIA *looks around her, trying to speak; can't.*)

(*Removing hat*) What is the matter with you people? Eh? You look like guests at a funeral . . . Sophia Yegorovna and I have just put on a perfect little comedy for you and you can't raise a single titter.

(SOPHIA *laughs, delighted at the relief.*)

Look at 'em, Sophia, I swear they've been embalmed . . .
(*Laughter, lifting and swelling, as they take the bridge he's offered to safer ground.*)

SASHENKA: (*Proud, apologetic*) My Misha can't bear it when things are calm . . .

SERGEI: Bravo, Misha, he's right, it's exactly what we deserve, he's the only one of us who dares live to the hilt, bless him. Without Platonov we'd all just . . . wither away completely . . .

TRILETSKI: Brilliantly put, Sergei Pavlovich. And on the subject of withering away, perhaps we could prevail upon our good hostess to furnish a little sustenance before too long . . . I could eat a pig whole. Your Excellency, I beg of you . . .
(*He smiles down the terrace at* ANNA. *She sits unsmiling a moment. Rises.*)

ANNA: How impudent and tiresome you have become, Nikolai Ivanovich. Everyone else waits, why shouldn't you? How can you be hungry? When are you ever not hungry? You spend your whole life gorging yourself. This morning what did you have, hunh? Two glasses of tea, a mound of beef, five eggs . . .

TRILETSKI: . . . Four . . .

ANNA: Five, I watched you, amazed. Then you stole into the larder and demolished half a pie. I've had no peace since daybreak with your guzzling and your shouting . . .
(*Sounds off, people on the approach.* ANNA's *wholly convincing display of patrician temper finds a new gear.*)
. . . What in God's name is all that noise? Stop it, damn you, stop that din . . .
(*She walks forward to the edge of the veranda; stares down the garden fiercely; softens slowly, as the voices advance.*)
Aha. Eh voilà. My hero. Mon chevalier!
(SHCHERBUK *appears, toils up the garden, mid-tirade. He's fifty or so, burly, sweating in the sun, voice habitually and crakingly over the top. His nephew,* PETYA, *ten, in white uniform and shiny-peaked hat, straggles disconsolately behind him.*)

SHCHERBUK: (*From off*) . . . I shall be watching you, my boy, be in no doubt about that. Put but a word or muscle out of place and by God you will pay for it, yes indeed . . . And I want that suit as spotless when we leave as when you put it on this morning . . .

ANNA: (*From terrace steps*) Pavel Petrovich!

SHCHERBUK: (*Puffing up*) I've had to bring my nephew, no one to look after him, my daughters have gone off somewhere in their ludicrous green gowns, they look like toads, lizards . . .
(*He bows, kisses her hand, waves at the others assembling behind her.*)

ANNA: Now here is a real character, realer than any of you . . .

SHCHERBUK: Petya, he's called. (*To boy*) Pay your respects to her Excellency.

PETYA: *Bonjour, madame.*

ANNA: *Bonjour, petit.*

PETYA: Congratulations on your marriage.

(ANNA *laughs.* SHCHERBUK *clatters the back of the lad's head, spilling the cap.*)

SHCHERBUK: It's her son who's married, not her Excellency, you don't listen . . . Pick it up, boy.

(*The lad collects his hat, raw-eyed, as* SHCHERBUK *exchanges greetings with the company.*)

And where, my friends, might she be, the one my soul burns to see . . . ?

(SERGEI *and* SOPHIA *stand by the house door.* ANNA *beckons them forward.*)

ANNA: Pavel Petrovich Shcherbuk, friend, neighbour, admirer and creditor . . .

SHCHERBUK: . . . Not to mention close companion of his Excellency, the late General. May I?

(*He bows to kiss* SOPHIA'*s hand. She pulls it away.*)

SOPHIA: Thank you, that really isn't necessary.

(SHCHERBUK *stares, frowns.* SERGEI *puts his arm round* SOPHIA'*s shoulder.*)

SERGEI: I trust you're not offended, honoured sir. It's just that in our view handkissing demeans women. We don't kiss men's hands now, do we? And we're opposed to all forms of inequality, inequality being, of course, the first step towards humiliation . . .

(SHCHERBUK *sniffs, looks briefly around, sees the boy on the garden steps.*)

SHCHERBUK: What are you then, Sergei, her lawyer? (*To* PETYA) Go and play. There's a lake over there. Stay out of it.

(*The boy shuffles off.* SHCHERBUK *returns to the fray with relish.*)

Aha, what have we here? Liberals, is it? Humanists, progressives, your heads full of shallow nonsense, hunh? Liberty, Equality, Fraternity, Hogwash. Me? I'm a Darwinist, pure and simple. I have science behind me when I say that blood and breeding will decide the fate of the species. Noble blood equals pure breeding. Q.E.D. Not empty words, I assure you . . .

(*People have relaxed back into the veranda terrace.* PETRIN *has resumed his silent reading.* SASHENKA *has recovered her straw*

hat, is trying to get it to sit straight on her brow. TRILETSKI
watches ANNA, *who has her arm inside* SHCHERBUK'S.
PLATONOV *appears at the house window, discreetly knocking
back another chaser.* SHCHERBUK *barristerially releases the
pinned pair, wanders a little, addressing the jury.*)
Equality. I ask you. Was it some scummy peasant who gave
us art, music, literature, science . . . ? You think a bunch of
wet-arsed slugs created Petersburg, do you? Ha!
(SERGEI *tries to think of the answer. Goes to speak;* SOPHIA *tugs
him to heel.*)

PETRIN: (*As if surfacing*) 'Hailstones the sizes of duck eggs fell on
Kostowata last week during a storm . . .'

SHCHERBUK: Gerasim Kusmich, we are talking here, and you
read aloud, hunh?
(PETRIN *stares at him calmly, gives him a thin smile.*)
So, my friends, by *not* associating with scum, by *not* shaking
their paws or inviting their snouts to my table, I further the
laws of natural selection . . . In other words, I do my duty
. . . (*He darts forward suddenly, kisses* SOPHIA'S *hand. Laughs
delightedly.*) Tell me honestly, does that demean you? I think
not. After all: Quod licet Jovi non licet bovi. What befits
Jupiter does not necessarily befit a bull, eh?
(PLATONOV *has returned from within.* SOPHIA *sees him
watching her.*)

SOPHIA: Perhaps you'll pay us a visit one day, Pavel Petrovich,
and we can argue the matter out . . .

SERGEI: Excellent idea. Together we will find the truth.

COLONEL: (*In his sleep*) Kalitin's bird dog farts when it points . . .
Gives the game away . . .
(*Laughter.*)

SASHENKA: Papa, please, sleep inside if you must, it's so
embarrassing.

COLONEL: (*Awakening*) . . . Wide awake, my love, wide awake.
What's the matter, mm?
(*Silence.* ANNA *surveys the company coolly, as vacancy settles
across them.* YASHA *has appeared at the upper balcony, the
telescope to his eye.*)

YASHA: (*Calling*) Zakhar and the other one have just crested the

ridge, madame. By my calculation, they should be here
within the next half hour . . .

ANNA: (*Staring up*) Who said you could handle the General's
telescope?

YASHA: How else am I to keep you posted?

ANNA: Put it back. At once.

(YASHA *glares a moment, stifflegs into the house. A crash.
Silence.*)

A little lunch, I think.

(*She leads off indoors;* SHCHERBUK *gives her his arm.*
TRILETSKI *follows* SERGEI *and* SOPHIA. SASHENKA *trundles
her father in, waves anxiously at* PLATONOV *as she passes him in
the doorway.* PLATONOV *stands for some moments; moves slowly
forward to the veranda terrace steps; stares out at nothing for a
long time. Is drawn eventually by sounds from the garden.*)

PLATONOV: Who is it? Who's there?

(*Young* PETYA *sits up in the hammock, face greasy with tears.
Silence.*)

Are you hungry?

(*The kid stands, shakes his head.*)

How about a swim? No? (*Thinks.*) Can you ride a bicycle?

(*The kid nods, interested.*)

There's one in the big barn . . . Over there.

(*The kid sniffs, straightens his peaked cap, salutes, marches off
for the barn.*)

(*As if to the kid*) Better still, bring the horse and carriage,
we'll run away together . . .

(*A* SERVANT, *just entered the garden to clear away, overhears
him, looks around for whom he might be addressing.*)

(*Quiet, as if cheery*) It's all right. I'm just going mad.

(*The* SERVANT *nods, satisfied.* PLATONOV *very slowly slides to a
sit on the top step. Silence.* SOPHIA *steps silently out on to the
veranda, approaches the rail to one side of the steps, turns her
back to the garden, careful they should not appear to be
together.*)

SOPHIA: Mikhail Vasilyevich. May I speak with you?

(*He nods, not looking.*)

I need to apologize for my idiotic behaviour just now, that

. . . stupid interrogation. I'll perfectly understand if you feel too angry with me to discuss it.

(*He says nothing.*)

Do you?

PLATONOV: Not at all. (*Looks at her.*) There was a time. Not now. (*She looks at him, looks away at once. A river boat sounds a deep horn a mile away. Another answers.*)

SOPHIA: Where do they go? The boats?

PLATONOV: To paradise. Forgive me, that was puerile, I don't know where they go.

(*Voices lift suddenly in laughter, upstairs in the dining room beyond the balcony. She hears her name spoken.*)

SOPHIA: I wish there was somewhere we could talk . . .

PLATONOV: (*Wholly separate tack*) The landing pier. Remember?

SOPHIA: What? No, I meant here, now . . .

PLATONOV: The boat. The evening boat, what was it called?

SOPHIA: The boat? I . . .

PLATONOV: The old man with the banjo, the evening steamer, what was it called . . . ?

SOPHIA: Mikhail, please . . .

PLATONOV: *Aurora*. Of course. (*Looks at her again.*) Why have you come looking for me? What do you want? Of me? Have you forgotten the lake too? The dog . . . ? Under the bench? The boy crouched by the bridge with his fishing-rod . . . ?

SOPHIA: Stop, Mikhail . . . Your voice . . . You have quite misunderstood me . . . Sh.

(*She freezes. PLATONOV turns to look. ANNA has appeared in the downstairs window, helps herself to a large glass of Madeira. She's inward, functional; sees nothing. Tidies her hair, squeezes lemon on her neck. Leaves the frame.*)

(*Eventually, her back still to him*) My God. She might have seen us. My God.

PLATONOV: And the fog. Rolling in from the sea. Remember? People disappearing . . .

SOPHIA: I beg you, no, no, it's not this I want, I've misled you . . .

(*Voices, laughter again above. She rubs her face, searches for words.*)

22

Mikhail Vasilyevich, the past was beautiful, extraordinary, I recall everything and regret none of it . . . I can see him now, the old you, Misha with the panama hat and the armful of books and the pockets bulging with tobacco . . . but you're a schoolmaster now, with a wife and a child, and I'm Sophia Yegorovna Voynitseva, wife to Sergei, the two of us dedicating our lives to useful work . . .

(*She talks softly, her back still to him.* PLATONOV *has sat motionless, eyes on the garden.* PETYA *has returned, stands staring at* PLATONOV, *his hands supporting the bicycle.* PLATONOV *stands slowly, glides into the garden, makes a weird shuffling beeline for boy and bike.*)

(*Unaware*) . . . We must let the past remain just that. A young student loved a girl, the girl loved him, it's too trite a story to disturb us now . . .

(PLATONOV *has reached the bike and straddled it. Lifts the kid into the front basket. Wobbles unsteadily off.*)

Say I'm right, Misha.

(*Silence. She turns for his answer. Finds nothing. Works on her hurt and anger. Jumps at the voice behind her.*)

SERGEI: (*Arriving from house*) Sophia, my love, I just had this amazing thought and wanted to share it with you . . .

(PLATONOV *wobbles back into the garden. The kid shrieks his pleasure.*)

(*Calling*) Watch out, Misha, Mama's looking for you . . .

(PLATONOV *waves, the bike veers wildly, he rights it and disappears again.* SOPHIA *watches, a touch bitterly.*)

. . . The thing is, Germany or Belgium are little places, mm? And the closer people are, the faster new ideas can be spread from one to another. Holland and England are the same, but here the country is so vast, in bad weather we can hardly reach our neighbours, let alone the people in Kamchatka or Siberia . . .

SOPHIA: . . . Sergei.

SERGEI: Yes, my love.

SOPHIA: Let's have some wine.

SERGEI: What?

SOPHIA: Some wine.

SERGEI: Of course, of course . . .

(*He puts his arm around her shoulder, leads her in.* ANNA
appears on the balcony, scans the garden.)

You know, I am so happy, Sophia. Voltaire, you, Mama . . .
My cup runneth over . . . Really.

(*They enter the house.* ANNA *calls* 'Mikhail Vasilyevich' *twice,
re-enters the dining room.* PLATONOV *reappears, wiping dirt
from his trouser leg; settles into the hammock; uses a stick to keep
it swaying.* ANNA *leaves the house.* YASHA *follows her out. The
afternoon light has begun to dribble away.*)

ANNA: Mikhail Vasilyevich.

(PLATONOV *waves the stick above the hammock.*)

YASHA: I shall need your instructions for dinner, madame.

ANNA: Have we heard from the gypsies?

YASHA: Er. No, madame.

ANNA: Send Mitka to the station with another telegram. And go
out yourself and hurry Zakhar in, they're holding things
up . . .

(*He goes to protest, she's down the steps and headed for*
PLATONOV. *The boy has returned, stands on the edge, peering at*
PLATONOV *in the hammock.*)

(*Arriving; seeing him*) Go and play.

(*The kid vanishes.*)

So. Are you by any chance avoiding me?

PLATONOV: Does the earth avoid the sun?

(*Silence. She thinks about that.*)

ANNA: Is that yes or no?

PLATONOV: Never mind. What is it?

ANNA: Porfiry Semyonovich has asked me to marry him.

(*Silence.* PLATONOV *rocks on.*)

PLATONOV: All winter long we yearn for the sun, when it comes
we can't bear it and want it gone.

ANNA: Did you hear me? He wants me to marry him . . .

(YASHA *walks past them, fuming, buttoning a coat. Disappears.*)

. . . It's tempting, I'll tell you. I could be rich overnight, pay
off all my creditors, Petrin, Shcherbuk, Kalitin . . . aiiee! I
could even put something into your schoolhouse . . . All I'd
have to do is learn to mow. Seems a small price to pay. Oh

24

and enter a loveless marriage. (*She looks at him.*) I'd like to
know your feelings. Can I stoop so low?

PLATONOV: (*Casual*) Oh, I should think so.

ANNA: If this is a joke, Misha, shouldn't one of us be laughing by
now? Are you trying to be rid of me, is that it? Move over.
(*She pushes his legs, he swings them to the ground, she sits next to
him.*)
I know we haven't seen each other all winter . . . but if you
have problems, let me know them, mm? Just don't play the
fool with me, Misha. Not me.

PLATONOV: I don't know. You're bright and good and lovely,
Anna, and worthy of . . . better than this . . . (*He waves a
hand at the hopeless terrain.*) Let's put the past behind us.
Let's just be friends. Your future's yours to decide, no one
else's . . . Besides, I'm just a touch married myself . . .
(*Silence. Sounds of grunting and straining off.*)

ANNA: Your wife is irrelevant, Misha, why raise her now? You
think I'm blind? It's that bloody Sophia, isn't it? You want
to tell me what's going on, mm? You don't have to be
ashamed, my dear, no one knows better than I what a sewer
rat you are, au fond . . . Without me, you'll drown, Platonov.

PLATONOV: Oh God. Ten years from now we'll sit in our
deckchairs and chuckle till we weep at all this. And a thick
fog will cover everything . . .

YASHA: (*Arriving unheard behind them, a garden chair in his hand*)
. . . Not quite everything, there will always be Yasha,
Excellency . . .
(*He's setting his chair before them and is halfway to the sit.*)

ANNA: (*Fierce*) Who gave you leave to speak, you oaf!

YASHA: (*Rising, retreating with chair*) You told me to tell you when
the surprise arrived, it's here, forgive me for breathing . . .
(*RADISH and ZAKHAR have struggled on by a side path with the
wrapped load.*)
. . . As for oafs, that doctor friend of yours is a bigger one, he
set fire to Mr Petrin's newspaper. (*Cackles maniacally*) While
he was reading it!

ANNA: Out of my sight!
(*The peasants lay the load down in the garden, slump to earth,*)

drained. SHCHERBUK *leads the* COLONEL *and* TRILETSKI *out on to the balcony, their wine glasses in their hands.*)

SHCHERBUK: . . . There's no case for mixed breeding, none whatsoever. Richard the Lionheart had the heart of a lion, yes? But where did it come from, if not his noble and valiant parents . . . Breed with scum and you'll get scum for your litter . . . Aha, there it is, the surprise. Intriguing . . .

COLONEL: (*Peering*) What is it, a cannon? If it's a cannon, I'll drink to it.

SHCHERBUK: (*Clinking glasses*) You'll drink to it anyway, Colonel . . .

ANNA: (*Sotto; still by* PLATONOV *in the hammock*) You must be losing your mind, Platonov. You have me. Isn't that enough? (*She leaves the hammock abruptly, clapping her hands and calling as she heads up the garden.*)

Everyone out of doors, if you please, it's time for the surprise I promised . . .

(*Behind her, the hammock has swung violently, pitching* PLATONOV *to the ground. He scrambles up quickly, trying to cover the embarrassment. The three men on the balcony disappear indoors.* ANNA *stops midway to instruct the loadbearers. They struggle to their feet, caps in hand, to listen. People begin to drift out on to the terrace, some still busy on the cold collation.* PLATONOV *tidies himself as he moves up the garden to join them. He glances in* ANNA's *direction as he passes her; she ignores him, goes on instructing the two peasants in idiot-English.*)

SOPHIA: (*Linking arms with* SASHENKA) . . . I really do love children, you know. And hearing you talk so warmly about yours has given me a splendid idea . . . Listen, everyone, if you'd be so kind, I'd like you all to hear my plan.

(SHCHERBUK *leads the* TRILETSKIS *out on to the terrace; they form, with* SASHENKA, SERGEI *and* PORFIRY, *a sort of arena for the announcement.*)

Tomorrow, my friends, I shall go to the village and arrange the bottle-feeding of all those babies whose mothers are at work in the fields. I would like to ask now for volunteers to assist me. Sashenka, say you will come . . .

(SASHENKA *looks to* PLATONOV *for guidance: he frowns.*)

Anna, what about you?

ANNA: (*Arriving; curt*) Sorry, I shan't be up until noon at the earliest . . . Yasha!

(SOPHIA *scans the watching group for support.* SERGEI'*s eyes brim with love and admiration.* PLATONOV *looks on darkly.*)

SOPHIA: Well, perhaps we could go to bed early . . . ?

ANNA: Out of the question, the gypsies are coming, Yasha . . .

(*He arrives, stonefaced, a tray in his hand.*)

There you are. The chairs, man, the chairs . . .

(*She begins showing him the arrangement she requires. The others direct their attention to the object down the garden, where* RADISH *and* ZAKHAR *have begun loosening the cowhide wrapping.* PETYA *has reappeared; tries to help.*)

SHCHERBUK: (*Calling*) Hands off, brat. Never touch what isn't yours.

ANNA: (*Sotto, to* YASHA) You've been at my drink again, haven't you . . .

YASHA: (*Above it*) I haven't touched madame's spirits, stealing is beneath me . . .

ANNA: Liar.

SOPHIA: I hope to meet your son one day. Your wife has told me miraculous things about him.

PLATONOV: She makes them up. All kids are the same, it's only the parents who differ.

SHCHERBUK: Not at all. Different parents breed different offspring . . .

ANNA: (*To the company*) Enough! Take your seats, if you will . . . Yasha, go.

(*People sit or stand, form a loose line along the veranda.* YASHA *leaves haughtily, drops the tray just inside the door, his hand grabs it as it rolls back on to the terrace.*)

(*A handclap.*) Zakhar!

(*The two men strip the hide from the object. The company stares at a brightly burnished mahogany upright piano.*)

(*A handclap*) Chair!

(RADISH *carries a garden chair, sets it down before the keyboard.*)

SHCHERBUK: A piano? Where's the surprise in a . . .

ANNA: Sh. (*A handclap.*) Zakhar!

(ZAKHAR *looks at* RADISH, *smiles palely, wipes hands and feet, sits, lifts the lid, stares at the brilliant keys. Raises his hands above them.*)

Play!

(ZAKHAR'*s hands go down,* RACHMANINOV *swells and twirls around the garden. The terrace people watch as if tranced.*)

COLONEL: (*Peering*) It's not a cannon at all.

SHCHERBUK: This is not possible. Not possible.

ANNA: Zakhar!

(ZAKHAR *stands, bows, edges nervously away from the still-playing pianola. The terrace people stand paralysed, deep in the event, nervous uncertainty edging towards fear.* ANNA *takes them in one by one, enjoying herself. Thunder; closer.* SASHENKA *sways, grows unsteady; slumps finally in a faint across the balustrade.* SOPHIA *moves to help her,* PLATONOV *is balked by the* COLONEL, *curses as he rounds him.*)

SOPHIA: Take her indoors, please, I have some drops . . .

SHCHERBUK: Leave her, she needs air.

(PLATONOV *moves her to a chair, crouches anxiously to look at her, rubs her hands in his.*)

SASHENKA: (*Reviving*) Forgive me, Misha.

PLATONOV: What's the matter with you? You're behaving like Anna Karenina . . .

SASHENKA: The heat, I grew frightened, and my head . . .

PLATONOV: Why come out with a headache in this heat? You could have stayed at home.

(*He tries to straighten her cock-eyed hat, she flinches away from him, tries to straighten it herself.*)

And take that off, will you, I can't bear the sight of it.

(SOPHIA *hurries forward with drops and water.* SASHENKA *removes the hat.*)

SOPHIA: Here, I have the drops, they're a little bitter but they're what you need . . .

PLATONOV: (*Exploding*) Are you just going to stand there, she's your sister, attend to her!

TRILETSKI: (*Pouring more wine*) Yes, yes, yes, yes . . . (*Moves forward to* SASHENKA *and* SOPHIA.) Now, what's the matter

28

with you, tubby? (*To* SOPHIA) What's that?

SOPHIA: Drops. I had them from my . . .

TRILETSKI: Drops? Ba. In the best circles one prescribes
sherry . . .
(*He holds his glass to* SASHENKA'S *lips, she chokes a little.*)
See. Better already.
(PLATONOV *grimaces, moves to the steps.* ANNA *has re-entered
the garden, closed down the music, gathers the piano-roll and
holds it above her head.*)

ANNA: See.
(*Some ragged laughter at the trick she's played.* SHCHERBUK
scowls, trying to smile.)

SHCHERBUK: Trickery! I said a peasant couldn't do it, didn't I?
It's beyond them. It's a machine, nothing more.

PETRIN: (*Approaching balustrade*) How much?

ANNA: Two thousand. Don't be so bourgeois.

PETRIN: Two thousand for a fainting fit? What do you say,
Platonov?
(PLATONOV *says nothing, walks into the house. People begin to
settle again on the terrace.* SOPHIA *stays with* SASHENKA, *eager
to nurse.* TRILETSKI *picks up a guitar, begins posing and
strumming between the tables.* PLATONOV *reappears in the
downstairs window, pouring a long drink of vodka.* SERGEI
moves forward suddenly to the edge of the terrace.)

SERGEI: Your attention, friends, if you please. As you know,
Sophia, my wife, plans to visit the village tomorrow to help
the peasant women. Well . . . I find that very inspiring.
Very. I believe she has shown us the way forward. And I
believe that we . . . the men . . . are honour bound to
respond. So. I have decided to give the peasants all my old
suits, every last one of them. And all my old shoes.
(*He gazes along the terrace at* SOPHIA, *who smiles a touch
unhappily, aware of the bored silence the announcement has
evinced. Thunder again, closing in still.* PLATONOV *begins
laughing in the window. Rolls out on to the terrace, the mirth
rising in desperate waves.*)

PLATONOV: . . . I just had this picture . . . of how extraordinary
they're all going to look . . . mowing in their frock-coats . . .

(He doubles up, close to explosion. Laughter ripples across the space, taking everyone in its path. Down the terrace, SASHENKA *turns in her chair to join in, happy he's happy.)*

SERGEI: *(Through laughter)* You know, that never occurred to me . . . That's very funny . . .

*(*SOPHIA *stands slowly, levels a bitter stare at* PLATONOV, *who hangs helpless over the balustrade, face greasy with tears; walks slowly into the house. Light very slowly fades. In the garden,* PETYA *has crept back to the pianola; he sits now, lid open, playing on air.)*

ACT TWO

Black. Thunder, rolling, dying. Sounds of voices, slow hammering.
Fade up: Garden, evening, light almost gone. Servants trail out from
the rear of the house to a long table being laid for dinner. Above, on a
crude ladder footed by ZAKHAR, RADISH *hammers up a waterproof*
awning over the dining area. YASHA *troops importantly in and out to*
supervise, holding the ring between kitchen and table.
Laughter, excited shrieks, off, from the house.

ANNA: (*Off, calling*) Come along, come along, am I to wait all
      night . . . ?

The casual, concrete images of invisible labour underpinning the life of
the house slowly crossfade to:
Veranda terrace, now beaded by small variously coloured overhead
lamps that give it a festive feel. The pianola stands against the house
wall, ready for use.
ANNA *sits at a green baize table; shuffles a deck of cards.* PETRIN *sits*
some distance away, reading a paper by lamplight.
More laughter from the house.
PETYA *appears on the balcony, lays his lamp on the balustrade, stands*
immobile, telescope to eye, staring into the far darkness. A train weeps
its way across country, miles away.
ANNA *walks casually along the terrace, stopping at tables to memorize*
the little stacks of playing cards already consigned to the game.
PETRIN *watches her; she ignores him.*

PETRIN: (*Reading*) 'A strike of all two thousand workers brought
        production to a standstill at the giant Putilov plant in
        Moscow yesterday . . .'
        (*Laughter again.*)
ANNA: Bring the wretches out! I'm growing bored here . . .
      (*The door opens, people spill out on to the terrace in a bubble of*
      laughter, dragging the COLONEL *and* PORFIRY, *the forfeit-*
      payers, with them. SOPHIA *and* SASHENKA, *in men's panamas*

and droopy Fu Manchu moustaches, parade the two men before ANNA's *table. Versions of applause from* PLATONOV, *in Sashenka's hat;* SERGEI *in brilliant silk peasant costume; and* TRILETSKI, *in false nose, spectacles and moustache.* ANNA *reviews the parade:* PORFIRY's *dressed and made up as a harem girl, the* COLONEL, *giggle-drunk, as a Moscow tart.*)

PORFIRY: (*Holding out his playing card*) Mercy, madame, have mercy, release me from this servitude, I beg you . . .

ANNA: Booboobooboo. You may return your card when you have danced with la jeune fille de Moscou. Allez, allez!
(*She claps her hands,* PETRIN *leans laconically forward beyond his paper to engage the pianola, which lurches clumsily into a polka.* PORFIRY *and the* COLONEL *fumble each other around the space, helplessly adrift from the music. Servants, laden, move by in the garden dark, glance blankly at the revel as they go. The dance ends; the* COLONEL's *spread across a table, his rouged and mascara-ed face garish in the beady light. Applause, help; cards are returned, the forfeits paid.* PETRIN *leans forward to disengage the pianola.* PLATONOV *and* SASHENKA *move to their table. He mops his face, with the band of Sashenka's hat; puffed.*)

SASHENKA: (*Full of him*) Mishenka, I'm so glad we're us. You're so . . . funny and clever and . . . oh everything. With you I'm so happy, so sure of things . . . You fill my days.
(*She kisses him, a sudden awkward lunge.*)

PLATONOV: (*Trying to disengage her arms*) Sasha, please . . . I'm hot enough as it is, there are people . . . You can do that at home.

ANNA: (*Piercing; missing nothing*) On, please. Sophia, your call.

SOPHIA: (*Taking proffered card*) Let me see, let me see. Whoever holds this card must . . . must . . .

SHCHERBUK: (*A bellow*) . . . ride a pig around the house!

SOPHIA: Precisely! The Knave of Spades!
(*The men ruffle through their cards.* SASHENKA *vets* PLATONOV's, *who stares darkly at* SOPHIA.)

TRILETSKI: (*Moving forward*) Je l'ai. C'est moi. (*A formal bow to* ANNA.) Let the pig be summoned.

ANNA: Sergei, tell Yasha to bring a pig! A quiet one, mind, one with a little grace, if you please.

(SERGEI *exits dutifully, blows a kiss back to* SOPHIA. *Laughter at something down the terrace.*)

Colonel! Enough.

(*The* COLONEL's *on all fours, grunting and squealing.*)

A pig has been sent for, you are de trop, sir.

COLONEL: Look no further, dear lady, ye'll find no finer pig in all Russia . . .

SASHENKA: (*Approaching to tend him*) Father, please, you'll tire yourself . . .

TRILETSKI: . . . God willing.

PLATONOV: (*Joining* SASHENKA) Come along, Colonel, we'll find you a nice sty upstairs . . .

COLONEL: Haven't had my supper . . .

PLATONOV: . . . We'll put some swill in a bucket for you . . .

(*The* COLONEL *waves them away, clambers mazily to upright, wades unaided to his chair with odd hauteur. Thunder.*)

COLONEL: See. Nothing.

(*He sits heavily. Giggles.* YASHA's *arriving from the house,* SERGEI *in his wake.*)

SERGEI: The idiot claims not to understand your instruction, Mother . . .

YASHA: . . . If it please your Excellency, the General's son here tells me I'm to embark on some polar expedition for a pig.

ANNA: (*Curt; ignoring him*) Yes? (*To guests*) Who's next?

YASHA: If you could but put yourself in my place, madame, you would see at once how unthinkable your orders are.

(*She looks at him curtly.*)

Who will serve your guests their dinner, do you imagine? The pig-ignorant Zakhar? The other one . . . ? Deaf Polya with the skin complaint . . . ?

ANNA: Send one of them then. See to it. (*To terrace*) Come along, who's left?

(YASHA *bows, edges off. Eventually speaks with* ZAKHAR, *who peels off into the night.*)

SERGEI: I haven't had a turn yet, Mother. And there's Shcherbuk . . .

SOPHIA: . . . I do believe Mikhail Vasilyevich has not yet been called . . .

SASHENKA: (*Moving forward*) . . . I haven't named a forfeit yet,
may I?

ANNA: (*Card in hand*) The card is drawn, my dear, I'm sorry, you
take the next one. Whoever has this card must come and kiss
me. (*She looks at it carefully.*) The Ace of Hearts.
(*Cards are checked; blanks drawn.*)

PORFIRY: Whoever has it, name your price, I'll buy it from
you . . .

SASHENKA: (*Checking Platonov's*) It's here, you have it, my love.
(*Holds it up.*) See, Anna. Now you must kiss my Misha.
(*She giggles, nervous.*)

PORFIRY: Mikhail, I beg of you, name your price . . .

ANNA: . . . You think my lips can be bought, sir? Enough. Come,
Monsieur Platonov. Pay your forfeit.
(ANNA *rounds the table, lays the card face down on the baize,
calmly awaits his approach.* PLATONOV *dwells a moment; moves
slowly forward. People watch intently. Mutters, whispers,
chuckles.* PETRIN *angles his paper a little to take it in. The two
face each other for some uneasy moments,* ANNA *amusedly
impassive,* PLATONOV *uncertain.* ANNA *carefully lays her arms
on his shoulders and draws his mouth to hers in a long and
increasingly intense embrace. Lifetimes elapse, stars die in the
silence.* PORFIRY's *crest, shaky at the best of times, slowly falls:
he collects a lamp and heads off unseen into the dark.* SASHENKA
*falters softly around the edge of things, an uncertain smile on her
lips, checking others' faces for reassurance it's just a game. The
smash of glass cuts the kiss, pulls all eyes down the terrace.*
PETYA's *telescope swings with them.* SOPHIA *stares at the debris
by her feet, looks up at the others.*)

SOPHIA: Forgive me. It slipped from my hand . . .

SERGEI: . . . It's a sign of good fortune to come, my love . . .

ANNA: Oh, I'm sure it is. (*Moving towards her*) Take care, you'll
hurt yourself . . . (*Shouts*) Yasha! (*Stoops to help her.*) Yasha
will look after it . . .
(YASHA *ghosts in, pulls a face.* PETYA *arrives on the terrace, sees
the excitement's died, heads petulantly for the gramophone.*)

YASHA: Leave it to Yasha, dear ladies. Yasha does everything . . .

34

SOPHIA: I can't think how it happened . . .

(PLATONOV *has moved to the garden steps, stares out at the night.* SASHENKA *edges towards him, stops some paces away. He sees her, looks at her sombrely for a moment; suddenly makes a face at her. She grins, winks at him, hugely relieved.* ANNA *has returned to the card table.* PETRIN'S *there before her, the forfeit card in his hand. He shows her the card: she gives him a blank cool look.*)

PETRIN: (*Soft*) The Ace of Hearts, hunh?

ANNA: (*As soft; a smile*) Tais-toi, mon vieux. (*To the gathering*) On, on. Who's next? Monsieur Shcherbuk . . . Entertain me. Something elevated, if you please . . .

(SHCHERBUK *moves reluctantly forward, pleased to be asked. A spatter of applause.* PLATONOV *pads off into the garden.* SOPHIA *watches him from the terrace rail.*)

SHCHERBUK: Well, I suppose I could give you something, a little impression I picked up from Prince Sergei Konyaev . . . His Excellency performs it far better than I do, of course . . . it's the mating call of the Siberian moose, King of the Forest, Monarch of the Glen. I shall need assistance and a few moments of preparation . . . Petya, you'll do for one . . . Now then, who else . . . ?

ANNA: (*A handclap at the passing* RADISH.) You there, what's your name, come and help monsieur . . .

(RADISH *lays down his ladder, approaches the terrace, cap in hand.*)

SHCHERBUK: Know how to whistle, d'ye?

RADISH: Whistle?

SHCHERBUK: Whistle, dummy, *whistle*. Like a bird, birdsong . . .

(RADISH *puts fingers to teeth, produces a perfect blackbird.*)

. . . Enough, fine, follow me, it's not your show, you know . . . Beggar thinks he's a genius. (*Over shoulder*) Amuse yourselves, dear friends, we shall return . . .

(*He leads peasant and boy away into the house.*)

ANNA: (*Handclap.*) Music. Let there be music.

(PETRIN *pushes the lever, the pianola sets up on a wobbly pavane, the group pair off into dance:* SERGEI *and* SOPHIA; SASHENKA *and her father.* ANNA *looks for* PLATONOV;

summons TRILETSKI. PLATONOV *stands mid-garden watching.
The great table is all but ready.* YASHA *surveys it, delicately
threading his fingers into white serving gloves. Thunder. A*
STRANGER *appears at the bottom of the garden, glasses, thick
moustache, begins the approach to the house.*)

YASHA: (*Seeing him*) You there, what's your business . . . ?

PLATONOV: (*To* YASHA) It's all right, I'll see to him. (*To*
STRANGER) Can I help?

STRANGER: (*Mud-spattered, tired from his trip*) My name's
Gorokhov, clerk at the timber mill, I need the doctor, I'm
told he's here . . .

PLATONOV: . . . Happy to meet you, Mr Gorokhov . . .

GOROKHOV: I doubt that. You're about as happy to meet Mr
Gorokhov as I am to be him. If you'll just . . .

PLATONOV: He's up there, the tall one . . .

GOROKHOV: Thank you.

(*The* STRANGER *heads for the steps.* PLATONOV *ambles after
him, amused; watches him remove his boots before taking the
steps, as the revellers whirl crazily past him. The clerk gazes at
the extraordinary scene a moment, crosses himself as if to ward off
the danger he senses.*)

COLONEL: (*Still the tart, en passant*) What is it? What d'ye want?

GOROKHOV: (*After him*) Name's Gorokhov. I'm looking for the
doctor. . .

(*People spin on past him.* TRILETSKI *hands* ANNA *to* PETRIN,
*approaches the steps. He still wears false nose, moustache,
glasses.*)

TRILETSKI: What is it?

GOROKHOV: It's my wife. It's all in here. (*He hands him a letter,
watches the whirl as* TRILETSKI *reads it.*) What is it,
spiritualism?

TRILETSKI: . . . Look, if this woman's your wife, what's the point
of a letter, why not just tell me?

GOROKHOV: I wasn't sure I'd be let in. I could've left the
letter . . .

TRILETSKI: Mm. Well, I'm afraid tonight's out of the question.
Tomorrow maybe. In the evening.

GOROKHOV: My boss has lent me transport, I could take you

there and back, couple of hours at the most . . . I can pay, I
have the money.

TRILETSKI: That's as maybe, tonight is not possible. Possibly
tomorrow. Day after at the very latest . . .
(*He tucks the letter into* GOROKHOV's *top pocket, his attention
already back on the dance. Thunder.*)

GOROKHOV: Your Excellency, please come with me, I beg of
you, sir, she's not well, she's . . .
(TRILETSKI *has removed the half-mask. The clerk reads the cold
eyes.*)
Forgive me, sir, I do understand. Please excuse me . . .
(TRILETSKI *returns to the revel.* GOROKHOV *sits on the bottom
step to draw on his boots. Sees* PLATONOV *approaching.*)
You might've told me the doctor was otherwise engaged,
now I've made him angry he may never come . . .
(*He stamps his boots on the grass, stumps off into the dark.*
PLATONOV *watches him a moment, as the music ends up above;
climbs up to the terrace.* TRILETSKI's *pouring himself a drink.*)

PLATONOV: The man's wife is sick, why didn't you go?

TRILETSKI: Oh Lord, here we go . . . spare me the bloody
sermon, will you? I am what I am and do what I do, just
leave me alone . . .

SASHENKA: . . . But if the woman's ill, Kolya, and you are here,
that's wicked . . .

TRILETSKI: (*Rounding on her*) . . . Who asked your opinion,
you're scarcely out of nappies?

PLATONOV: (*Huge; smashing table with fist*) Don't you dare speak
to my wife like that, you idle bastard! You're the only doctor
in the area, you swore an oath to tend the sick and the needy,
it's your moral duty to show compassion . . .

TRILETSKI: . . . All right, all right, you want me to go, I'll go.
Jesus. I'll have my dinner and then I'll go.
(*Silence.* PLATONOV *rubs a bruised fist, still seething; catches*
SOPHIA's *gaze, the new admiration there in the eyes; looks away,
finds* ANNA's *mocking face.*)
But while we're on the subject, dear friend, you're not
exactly the world's most dedicated schoolmaster either . . .

PLATONOV: (*A new fury*) Aha, so it's all my fault, I'm a lousy

37

teacher so you don't have to tend the dying, you're free to let 'em pop off while you souse yourself in booze, eh? Listen, friend, I left university before graduation, I gave my place to someone else, but you bloody didn't, so buckle to and do your duty . . .

(*An extraordinary mooing sound sets up down the terrace.* SHCHERBUK's *arrived, flanked by the twittering* RADISH *and the antler-bearing* PETYA, *giving them his celebrated Monarch of the Glen.* PLATONOV *sighs his exasperation. Glares across at* TRILETSKI. SHCHERBUK *dins relentlessly on.* TRILETSKI *grins nervously at* PLATONOV, *who softens to a chuckle. The company moves to laughter, another crisis negotiated.* PORFIRY *reappears at the garden steps; stares up at the weirdness above. Fade to black.*)

Trail, from darkness, sounds of people at table.

ANNA: (*Unseen*) Well, friends, this might be the appropriate moment for everyone to drink my health . . .

(*Fade up: Garden. Table. Night. Servants carry on more lamps, as the dinner progresses.* YASHA *serves more cutlets with finicky precision.* ANNA *heads the table,* PORFIRY *sits by her,* PLATONOV's *flanked by* SASHENKA *and* SHCHERBUK, *Sergei's seat at the foot is empty,* SOPHIA *beside it;* PETRIN *sits with* PETYA *facing* PLATONOV. *The low hum and chomp of people deep in a meal.*)

(*On; calling*) Sergei, for heaven's sake where are you?

SERGEI: (*Emerging from house, book in hand*) Coming, Mother . . .

COLONEL: (*Waking*) . . . This policeman claimed earthquakes are caused by evacuation . . .

TRILETSKI: . . . evaporation . . .

COLONEL: . . . Exactly. Some German discovered it. Said we must put our faith in haemorrhoids . . .

TRILETSKI: . . . Metalloids . . .

SASHENKA: Papa!

TRILETSKI: Go back to sleep, eh?

COLONEL: Don't make fun of me, boy. Maybe I'm alive today because I sleep so well . . .

SERGEI: (*In his chair, search over*) Found it! I knew it was in here. Listen everyone . . . 'Russia is a vast unending plain on which only men of courage and character may stand.' There.

SHCHERBUK: (*Spraying food from stuffed cheeks as he speaks*) Yes, and who are these men of courage and character, pray? (*He stands awkwardly, wine-sodden. No one pays him much heed, used to him.*)
Blue-bloods, that's who! Whatever's good, whatever's *best* on this earth is the work of the aristocrat. Absolutely. But today what do we do, mm? We smile on every kind of riff-raff. Kulaks, bottle-washers, clerks and postmasters, no ideas, no ideals . . . Civilization itself is under threat. Like germs, the scum will gobble everything they touch. Peasants, shopkeepers, scum everywhere, as far as the eye can see. Where are the blue-bloods now, eh? Where are your Pushkins, your Lermontovs, your Gogols and Goncharovs, mm?

PLATONOV: (*Factual*) Goncharov was a merchant, wasn't he?

SHCHERBUK: (*Unstoppable*) The exception proves the rule, my friend. Always. Not that Goncharov's genius is unassailable either . . . (*Resuming*) Plague and pestilence stalk the land, friends, and our duty to the race is clear. Unite, while we may, and deal the common enemy a mighty blow. Let me appear before this rising scum not as Pavel Petrovich Shcherbuk but as Richard the Lionheart.
(PETYA *slides slowly under the table, as his uncle screeches on.*)
All our kindness and sensitivity, where has it got us with these degenerates, eh? It's time to speak out clearly, straight to their ugly faces: 'Know your place, you rabble.' Pah. (*A spitting sound.*) Straight in their ugly mugs . . .
(*He sits heavily, drunkenly pleased with his oration.* SOPHIA *gives* SERGEI *the hard eye, pressing him to rebut.* SERGEI *clears his throat unhappily, not up to the task. The* COLONEL *chunners, head on the table.* TRILETSKI *gently strokes the old man's head.*)

PETRIN: (*Casual; from nowhere*) Fine. But count me out of it, all right?
(*Silence.* SHCHERBUK *blinks at him across the table.*)

SHCHERBUK: Really? And why is that, pray?

PETRIN: (*Calm, objective*) Because my father was a worker and his a serf. And if anyone here finds that unpalatable, I'm perfectly happy to leave. But just bear in mind, will you, that what you've eaten and supped here tonight was bought from my pocket. And the fireworks, mm? And the gun, the piano? I'm the reason you people survive. It's scum like me keeps you afloat. All you're fit for is preaching to others, how they should live, what they should believe. But what about your own lives, your own beliefs, what are they? Pavel Petrovich Shcherbuk, the mighty Lionheart, son of aristocrats, proud to be a blue-blood . . . but what use are you to anyone? You think the world's prepared to go on feeding you for ever because you've blue blood in your veins? What do you actually *do*, mm? The mating call of the Siberian moose? (*He moos softly, horns his fingers around his head, chuckles, rises from the table, takes out a good cigar, heads for a lamp on a side table to light it.*) Believe me, friend, the world has no need of you. These days, the world needs scum. I'm scum . . . nice word, eh? . . . and I can turn my hand to anything. My dad was terrified of this place, wouldn't come near it. And I've sat in every room in the house exchanging pleasantries with her Excellency. Not bad.

(*He lights his cigar carefully at the lamp. The table bears the weight of his meaning.*)

PORFIRY: (*Eventually*) Gerasim, Gerasim, what's got into you, my friend, talking like that in another's home, it's not right . . .

(PETRIN *smiles, unapologetic.* PLATONOV *slices a cutlet, forks a piece into his mouth.* ANNA *sips her wine, impassive. The* COLONEL *snores and snuffles a little.*)

SOPHIA: (*Nervy; keen to normalize*) Dear Gerasim, would you do me a great kindness and deal with that lamp, it's smoking, do you see? If there are two things in the world I cannot bear, it's draughts and smoking lamps . . .

(*Silence.* PETRIN *produces a penknife, begins trimming the wick.*)

PETRIN: (*Soft*) I bought the oil too.

ANNA: (*Sharp*) Eat. Everybody eat.

SHCHERBUK: (*Lurching upright again*) Thank you, I ate before I
came, I haven't touched a morsel . . .
(*He begins to walk away, struggling for a dignity he can't quite
achieve.*)
PLATONOV: (*Laying fork down*) Excellent. Really good.
(*The swoosh of a needle groping for a groove, Caruso full belt
from the terrace gramophone: 'Una Furtiva Lacrima'. Hearts
stop, small shrieks bubble to lips, heads swivel up the garden.
PETYA stares at them from the terrace, a defiant smile on his
face.*)
SHCHERBUK: (*Released into fury*) You little monster! Let me get
my hands on you, I'll give you the braying of a lifetime . . .
(*He rips a switch from the garden, lumbers after the already
fleeing boy, cuts the record* en route *for the house. The din of the
chase persists for a while, dies. Silence.*)
PORFIRY: (*Gently, his hand on* ANNA's) My dear lady, pay him no
heed, what Petrin says is of no importance . . .
ANNA: (*Removing her hand; pitiless*) Porfiry Semyonovich, you're
old enough to know better, make-believe will get us nowhere
. . . The General's wife was one thing, the General's widow is
quite another. Let me look askance at any creditor, I'll be
out of this house before I can say booboo . . . I've known it
for years: the estate or my honour. I chose the estate.
Gerasim Kusmich Petrin is a man of courage. And character.
And great wealth. He could sink me without trace. Instead,
he keeps me afloat. (*Raises her glass to* PETRIN.) Your health,
sir.
(PETRIN *smiles, makes an ironic formal bow.*)
PORFIRY: Dear Jesus, how painful it all is.
SERGEI: You see, Sophia? Poor, sad, unending Russia . . .
PLATONOV: (*A sudden spit*) Jesus God, leave Russia out of it, will
you?
SERGEI: I only meant to say . . .
PLATONOV: . . . You've been only meaning to say for fifteen
bloody years, man. Give your mouth a rest. Talk, talk, talk
. . . The Russian soul, the common weal, our hopes and fears
. . . it's a wonder our tongues haven't shrivelled with it all.
You yap on about Russia, Shcherbuk about scum, Porfiry

41

about love and chivalry . . . and flies wither on the wing from our wise pronouncements. Talk, eat, sleep, talk, talk some more, talk and more talk, all with a clear conscience. The only thing we take from the modern world is our sense of self-importance, everything else about us is back with the neanderthals . . .

SOPHIA: . . . How can you can say such things? It's disgraceful, it's immoral . . .

PLATONOV: (*Fierce*) What is? Recognizing one's own mediocrity? Well, what about bottle-feeding village infants and handing out frock-coats to their fathers? You don't find *that* just a touch immoral . . . ?

SERGEI: Ding dong ding dong, there's no stopping you, is there? You're like a church bell . . .

PLATONOV: . . . We're all like church bells, friend. The difference is, I toll only what I myself feel; for you, any cause at all can start your clapper banging . . . You've been down from university what, three years? And what do you do? Nothing. And what d'you plan to do? Nothing . . .

SERGEI: . . . I'm not starving, I've a long life ahead of me, what's the hurry . . . ?

SASHENKA: Stop, Misha, stop. You're wearing everyone down, my love . . .

PLATONOV: (*Standing, suddenly unsteady*) . . . Then don't listen, my darling. Sleep, like your papa there. He hears nothing. That way he can go on loving us all . . .

TRILETSKI: What has the old man ever done to you, eh? Have a go at me if you like, leave him alone . . .

PORFIRY: (*Standing*) He's not interested in the argument, he's just looking to show us how clever he is. They can't afford servants any longer, he has to find someone else to vent his spite on . . .

(*A weird yowling noise from the darkness. Heads turn, eyes peer.*)

ANNA: Now what?

YASHA: (*Looming*) The beast has arrived, your Excellency.

ANNA: What?

(ZAKHAR *looms behind him, a black and white sow in his arms.*)

42

YASHA: The pig, madame. For Mr Triletski, I believe.
  (*Relieved laughter, applause: another crisis bridged.*)
ANNA: Perfect! Enough philosophizing, Kolya's forfeit is to hand.
  Come, sir!
PLATONOV: (*Ambling away*) Fine. The pig's here. Go to it,
  learned doctor.
TRILETSKI: (*Rage and pain growing*) You go to hell, Platonov!
  What do you take me for, a clown, is it? It's what you all take
  me for, isn't it? The perfect clown, the court jester. What do
  any of you know about me, mm? What do you know of me?
  (*He's close to tears; the rage turns inwards.*) Do any of you have
  any idea how bored I am in this wasteland, mm? I have no
  life here. Waking at night if a dog so much as mewls, for fear
  it's someone coming to drag me off to some sickbed.
  Clattering over dreadful roads with hopeless horses, knowing
  I'll find diarrhoea at the end of it, terrified it'll be cholera . . .
  Oh, the books I've read on cholera . . . and feeling nothing,
  not a thing, for those who have it. Choking on shame and
  fear and self-disgust, sickened by living and drinking the
  way I do . . .
  (*People watch him, horrified;* SERGEI *can't bear it, moves from
  the table to stand in the darkness.*)
  I turn my head and see the whole of my future behind me.
  It's so unbearable to know how little is possible, to know that
  nothing can ever really be changed . .
SASHENKA: (*In pain*) Kolya, please, I beg of you, do stop. All of
  you, please stop.
  (*PLATONOV has collected a guitar, now sits on the swing, begins
  a soft strumming. Lamps flick and splutter in the dark space.*
  TRILETSKI *wipes his eyes with a napkin.*)
YASHA: What shall we do with the beast, madame?
SERGEI: (*Erupting*) Take it away, just go, go!
YASHA: (*Standing his ground as he retreats*) I wasn't actually
  speaking to you, sir. It was her Excellency who ordered the
  pig . . .
  (*He mutters on as he and* ZAKHAR *move off. Platonov's guitar
  takes hold again.* ANNA *stands; scans the company; raises her
  glass.*)

ANNA: Well, I'll drink my own health.
(*She drains the wine, lays down the glass, leaves in silence for the house. Passes* SHCHERBUK, *switch still in hand, returning.* PETRIN *has moved softly forward from dark to light and taken Anna's chair at the head of the table.* SHCHERBUK *sees him, heads for Sergei's vacant seat by* SOPHIA.)

PETRIN: Imagine the irony. At precisely this moment, in some warm tropical place, a man sits by his canoe on a perfect white beach debating whether to go and get himself a banana. Mm.
(*Silence.* PLATONOV *strums on in the near-darkness of the swing.*)

PLATONOV: (*Eventually*) I came across a story recently, I don't remember where. Quite a short one, but rather good. About a girl who fell in love with a student, he with her. He'd read books to her, she loved to listen. Sometimes, at dusk, they'd go down to the river and watch the lights of the boats pass by. They sang together, dreamed, kissed, swore their love . . .
(*The table listens in silence.* SOPHIA *takes more wine,* SASHENKA *scans faces, uneasy again.*)

SASHENKA: Who is it by, Misha, the story?

PLATONOV: Don't recall. The girl wore her hair long then, below her ears, and always on her skin the smell of spring water, and life for them both seemed to unfold like some unending festival . . . dedicated by a kind world to honour their love. And they were happy. One day, she told him she had to go to St Petersburg for a couple of days. 'Do I have your leave?' she asked him. 'Of course,' he answered, 'but you will be missed . . .'
(SOPHIA *stands carefully, glass in hand, stares into the darkness at the storyteller.*)
She took the midnight train, he saw her off at the station, she hugged him tenderly, he squeezed her hands and spoke not a word, scared he would weep. He watched the tail-lights dwindling, mile after mile, and whispered, 'My dear good girl. My wondrous woman.'
(*Pause. His guitar chords fill the silence.*)

A day passed. Two. Five. A month. She didn't come back.
The student kept watch at the station, met trains, drank
vodka in the station bar. Finally he stopped going. Came to
his senses. Grew up. Became an ordinary person . . .
(*The chords end.* PLATONOV *sits, his face averted. Long silence.*
SOPHIA *drains her wine, gazes around her, as if trapped.*)

SERGEI: Terribly good story. Sounds like Uspenski . . . or
Leskov maybe . . . ?
(PLATONOV *turns slowly in the swing to face the table.* SOPHIA
*bangs her glass down, heads off for the house, in tears, a napkin
to her mouth.*)

SASHENKA: (*In tears herself*) Oh God, what have you done now,
Mishenka? Must you hurt *everybody* . . . ?
(*A rocket blasts into the sky from behind the house, bursts above
them, washes them in a strange pink glow. They stare up at the
night.*)

ANNA: (*Calling, from terrace*) Enough, my friends. Everyone to
the river. Magic time!
(*Black.*)

SASHENKA: (*Calling from the blackness*) See, Misha, see. Look
how beautiful they are . . .
(*The first of a series of brilliant flare-like explosions convulsing
their settled world order.* SOPHIA *moves quickly through empty
space, a lamp in her hand, spectral in the weird off-white glow.*
PLATONOV *appears in her wake: he wears a long off-white open
burberry, mid-calf, like a Long Rider's coat.*)

PLATONOV: . . . Wait. Listen. For Christ's sake, woman, hear me
out. Please . . .
(*She stops, half turns. He gulps for air. They stare at each other
across the ghostly space.*)
Dear, wonderful woman . . . My life's gone, I know it, but
yours? What's become of *you*? Mm? Where's that . . .
simplicity and . . . spirit, unh? Where has all that gone
to . . . ?

SOPHIA: Stop. You're a wild man, you're out of control . . .

PLATONOV: . . . All right, but be honest with me, in the name of
what we once had, why did you marry this man?

45

SOPHIA: I married him because he's a fine person . . .

PLATONOV: . . . He's a *nothing*, and you know it . . .

SOPHIA: . . . He's my husband.

PLATONOV: You could have married *anyone*. You could have married someone with drive and courage and imagination, instead you choose a pygmy, soused in debt and paralytically idle. Why, my love? Why?

SOPHIA: Oh God. Please, Mikhail Vasilyevich, I beg of you, don't destroy my life again, laugh at me if you want, deride me, think of me what you will, but this is the only life I have now . . . There's nothing else. Nothing.

(*The flare fades fast: she stands in the blackness, lit only by her lamp.*)

Mikhail. (*Pause.*) Mikhail . . .

(*She takes a pace or two forward: he's gone. She stands for several moments as if dead, eyes closed, a slight post-mortem tremor in the limbs.*)

PLATONOV: (*From behind her*) How I loved you. My God, how I loved you . . .

(*Another great explosion, another great flare of spectral light washing the space. She turns, moves towards him; he wraps her tight in his arms.*)

(*Low, tiny voice*) Dear good girl. Wondrous woman. You know my problem? I believed in an afterwards. And life doesn't deal in such things. We kid ourselves that everything's still up ahead, waiting to be discovered, waiting to be lived, never mind what we do *now*, there's always 'later', there's always an 'afterwards' to put it right . . . And there isn't. There isn't. Back then . . . I didn't know that. I watched your train disappear . . . I *let* your train disappear. And . . .

SOPHIA: Oh God, my heart almost stopped when I saw you today . . .

PLATONOV: Remember the landing pier?

SOPHIA: Yes.

(*They move slowly into a kiss. At the point of closure, she pulls back with a tiny yelp.* PLATONOV *follows her gaze: sees* SERGEI, *cloak over arm, watching from a distance. Silence.*)

SERGEI: (*In shock; voice wobbling*) You asked for your cloak, my
love. I'm not here . . . on purpose. Purposely . . . You said
you were cold.
SOPHIA: Dear Lord. How banal.
(*She walks away; disappears.* PLATONOV *watches her go; turns
to face* SERGEI. *Silence. Flare fading.*)
SERGEI: (*Eventually*) I don't imagine you'll ever understand what
I'm . . .
(*He can't finish. Silence. It's almost black again.*)
Congratulations, Misha.
(*Another great explosion. Black. Slow soft flare across the empty
space. Black. Another.*)

Another flare washes the terrace. ANNA *sits in a chair, legs crossed,
foot swinging softly forward and back.* PORFIRY *kneels on one knee
before her, head slightly bowed, eyes fixed on the swinging ankle-boot,
rabbit to snake.*

PORFIRY: . . . At least give me some small hope, madame, some
glimpse of possible happiness, I don't say now . . . and I
don't ever expect you to . . . love me . . . as I love you but I
need meaning in my life. I need hope, Anna.
(*He looks up from foot to face.* ANNA *gazes blankly back at
him.*)
ANNA: And I, Porfiry, need time. You must try not to be selfish in
this matter . . .
SERGEI: (*Off, yelling, hopeless*) Maman, Maman, where are you, I
need you . . .
ANNA: (*Standing briskly*) Oh my God, what now? (*Calling*) Here,
boy, here!
(SERGEI *appears in the garden, dishevelled, distraught. Stops at
the foot of the steps.* PORFIRY *levers himself embarrassedly to
upright.*)
SERGEI: I need a horse, Maman.
ANNA: You need a horse.
SERGEI: I have to get away from this bloody place . . .
ANNA: Why, what has this bloody place been doing to you,
then . . . ? Is it me or is the whole world insane?

47

SERGEI: Maman, Anna, Maman, listen. I can't bear it. Tell me what I must do. I'm alone again. I'm on my own again. It's unbearable. Why me? Why me, Maman?

ANNA: (*Deliberately*) What. Happened? Has someone done something?

(*He lurches away; returns.*)

SERGEI: You're looking at a cuckold, Mother. Sergei Pavlovich Voynitsev: cuckold.

ANNA: (*Judging it*) Sophia?

(*He nods dumbly.*)

You caught her?

(*He nods again.*)

Platonov?

SERGEI: Sophia, Sophia, Sophia, Sophia, Sophia. Put me in an asylum, Mother, I'm the one who's insane, I still believe in love and truth and loyalty . . . Or just put me down, like a dog gone mad, no one needs me, I'm in the way . . .

(ANNA *opens her arms for him, he lumbers up the steps to her, she hugs him to her quite tenderly.*)

ANNA: . . . Boobooboo. Calm yourself. Everything will be as it was. Platonov doesn't need that silly little thing. He's far too sharp to fall for all that 'progressive' nonsense. Everything will be as it was, you'll see. Sophia will stay with you, Platonov with me, Sashenka with him . . .

(PORFIRY *recoils, handkerchief at mouth to stifle the horror. She doesn't notice.*)

Who needs this silly little flirt of a wife of yours, eh? Calmes-toi, enfant.

(SERGEI *has begun to pull away from her, horrified too. Flare fading.*)

SERGEI: How can you say such things, Maman? How can you?

(*He runs past her into the house.* ANNA *looks for* PORFIRY: *he's gone. Black, for a moment; another brief flare blossoms.* TRILETSKI *stands watching her broodingly from the garden steps.*)

ANNA: My physician. Boobooboobooo. Why so glum?

TRILETSKI: (*On the edge of something*) Excellency, I . . . Anna . . .

(*Silence. She laughs.*)

48

ANNA: (*Replicating his tone exactly*) Anna? Anna? It's a game, dear
   man. All of it. Who *ever* wants the one he may have? Sine
   qua non.
   (*Silence. He laughs; in pain. She begins to massage her shoulder
   by the neck. Light fading.*)
TRILETSKI: If I did not love you quite so much, madame, I
   believe I might find you rather hateful . . .
ANNA: (*A small laugh.*) No, you wouldn't.
TRILETSKI: (*Indicating her stiff neck*) Sometimes you hold yourself
   too tightly . . .
ANNA: I know.
   (*Black.*)

Another explosion, lighting the dining-room balcony. SASHENKA *and*
PETYA *stand hand in hand, marvelling at the brilliant sky.*
Black.

Explosion; flare over empty space. PLATONOV *appears at the trot,
knees bent, hands in the pockets of the long burberry, floating in weird
weaves across the terrain like a great bird, intoning a yadeda version of
'Una Furtiva Lacrima'. Stops. Stares.* PORFIRY *stands at the edge of
the space, a lamp in one hand, an uprooted sapling cudgelled in the
other, watching him.* PLATONOV *lights a cigarette. Coughs a little.*

PLATONOV: Is it me you want, old man?
PORFIRY: It is. I want to tell you, Mikhail Vasilyevich, how much
   I hate you. You are a knave, sir. You have destroyed my life,
   as you have destroyed others'. You hold the world in
   contempt and ridicule everyone in it save yourself. You
   scatter lust and faithlessness wherever you go and you do it
   with impunity. You go unscathed, yet you deserve to be
   broken, beaten to a pulp . . .
   (*He raises the sapling. Silence.* PLATONOV *draws on the
   cigarette; coughs again.*)
PLATONOV: You think life hasn't broken me too, old man?
   Nothing goes unpunished. But I'll tell you what: I don't give
   a weasel's tosser what you think of me. I know you decent
   honest folk. You're honest and decent because you haven't

49

got the guts or the imagination to be otherwise. Sinning's beyond you, you grow old and you can't get it up any more, hunh? So you turn your bile on those who still can . . .

(*They stare at each other for some moments, as if frozen. Flare slowly fading.* PLATONOV *glides suddenly forward, completes mazy surreal circles around the old man, yadeda-ing as he goes. Disappears. Light fades to black.* PORFIRY *raises his lamp, hurls the sapling after him with a dry scream, spits impotently several times in* PLATONOV's *general direction, finds most of the spittle lodged on his lapel, wipes it tearfully off with his free hand. Black.*)

SERGEI: (*Off, yelling*) Yasha. Zakhar, Mitka, where in God's name are you . . . ? Asleep, are you? Who gave you leave to sleep when you're needed, you lazy swine . . . ?

(*A whoosh; a flare floats briefly across the space.* SERGEI's *bent double, lugging a heavy travel trunk across the ground. Flare fading fast.*)

. . . When the General was alive you came all right, oh yes, at my beck and call you were then, the master's son, now you only answer to her . . .

(*Black again. Grunts, moans, sounds of a heavy fall. Servants run on in nightclothes:* YASHA, ZAKHAR, RADISH. *Their lamps reveal* SERGEI *on his face, the trunk upended, its contents spilled out on to the ground.*)

(*Screaming*) Where the hell's the horse I ordered? Where's my bloody horse?

YASHA: You don't have a horse, sir.

SERGEI: (*Hysterical*) Fetch me a horse. I want a horse. Here. Now.

(YASHA *looks at the other two; gives them a nod. They leave.* YASHA *takes a pace forward, shines his lamp on* SERGEI's *prone form.*)

YASHA: Might I suggest the young gentleman retires to his bed . . . ?

SERGEI: (*Full force still*) And where's my hat? Where the hell is my hat? I've looked everywhere . . .

(YASHA *stoops, pokes among the spillage from the trunk, locates the hat in question.* SERGEI *sits up, stares at the hat.* YASHA *leans forward, gently places it on* SERGEI's *head. Turns. Leaves.* SERGEI *weeps pathetically in the silent blackness. A flare briefly relights the space: he's trying to remove his wedding ring; can't budge it. Fade to black.*)

Wail of a slow train, a long way away.

PLATONOV: (*From the darkness*) Dearest Lord, how little one needs to be happy. To sit in a warm train, take tea by lamplight, idly chat with the chance fellow traveller opposite, headed somewhere, anywhere, but away from this miserable, this meaningless life. One thing I now know: only once betray, only once deny what you love and believe in, and the web of pretending and lying you spin will hold you fast for ever. Dearest Lord, save me, give me strength, show me a way.
(*The small bead-lamps on the terrace fade slowly up.* PLATONOV *kneels in the garden, mud-streaked, worn. Stands slowly. Slowly approaches the sleeping house. Climbs up to the terrace. Surveys the building. Approaches the door: finds it locked. Shivers in the pre-dawn cold.*)
SOPHIA: (*Soft, unseen*) I waited for you.
(*He turns. She's been crouched by the terrace rail; stands now; lays a tied bundle of clothes and belongings on a terrace table.* PLATONOV *stares at her wanly.*)
Come, Misha. We can go. You've brought me back from the dead. I'm happy again. And every day I will thank you for it. We'll start a new life, fresh as spring water, bright as the sun. We'll work till we drop and eat only the bread we earn, we'll find our joy in work and each other. Our lives will be a festival of truth and justice and honesty. You'll teach, I'll help you. We'll live simply, simple clothes, plain food. Come, Misha. Take me. (*She closes her eyes, extends her arm.*) Here's my hand on it. Feel it, it's frozen, I've waited so long . . .
(*She waits a little longer: nothing.* PLATONOV *tries the front door again. She opens her eyes.*)

51

Mikhail Vasilyevich . . .

PLATONOV: (*Slowly*) No, Sophia. No. It's no use. Won't
work . . .

(*He returns to the locked door, rattles the handle stubbornly. She
stares on at him. He turns round again to look at her; shakes his
head; resumes the pointless rattling.* SOPHIA *picks up her bundle,
takes the steps, falters a few paces into the near-dark garden. A
thin snoring sound meets her. She approaches quietly; makes out
the indistinct form of* SERGEI, *asleep on his trunk. She turns to
look at the house;* PLATONOV's *begun banging on the door; lays
down her bundle, sits on it. Lamps begin to blossom within the
house, voices rearing from sleep.* PLATONOV's *begun shouting, a
new incoherent fury building within him. Nightclad figures
appear in lamplight, above, below:* TRILETSKI *leans over the
upper balustrade, his father and* SHCHERBUK *in nightshirts behind
him.*)

TRILETSKI: What is it, Misha, what is it, are you hurt?

PLATONOV: (*Huge, hopeless voice*) I'm thirty-five years old, that's
what it is, I'm thirty-five years old and yes I'm hurt, I'm
hurt, I'm hurt . . . All gone. Thirty-five years, all gone, I'm
nothing, do you hear me?

(*He begins turning chairs and tables over, wrecking the terrace.
Screams from the house.*)

Thirty-five years of age and a complete nonentity!
Lermontov died at twenty-seven, Napoleon was already a
general, I've achieved nothing! Nothing! Sasha, where are
you? You've ruined my life, ruined it!

(SASHENKA *arrives on the balcony above, screams as she sees the
havoc.* PLATONOV *sees her.*)

I'm nothing because of you, d'you hear me? A useless,
worthless, hopeless nothing!

(SASHENKA *hurries indoors, calling his name.* PLATONOV
*smashes the pianola with his fists: a sort of crazy music leaps from
it, he throws himself blindly against it, kicking and yelling.*)

Stop it, stop it, you . . . machine, you . . .

(SASHENKA *arrives on the terrace. Others crowd after her. Pre-
dawn moves very slowly to dawn as they gather.*)

SASHENKA: Misha, I beg you, stop, please stop all this . . .

PLATONOV: (*Still blind*) Where's my mind gone? My strength? My talent?

(*She moves forward to restrain him. He sees her. Looks at his barked knuckles.*)

You're here too, are you? My keeper of the cold hearth. D'you know how much I despise you, eh? With your cabbage soup and your canaries. I know, you've nowhere else to go either. To see you day on day on day, to hear your silly voice and despise you almost as much as myself, and know nothing's possible . . .

(*She takes his hands, tries to draw him to her. For a moment he seems spent, then pushes her violently away.* TRILETSKI *catches her spinning tumble. Calls of* 'Shame!', 'Brute!', 'Shame on you.')

TRILETSKI: How dare you treat my sister that way? Who do you think you are, you louche uncouth bastard, you?

PLATONOV: (*Blinking; scanning the group*) I'm looking in a mirror. I'm just like the rest of you. A nothing.

(*A small movement by the door draws his eye.*)

It's all right, no need to leave, I'll do that for you . . . Wake you all up, did I? Ruined your beauty sleep, have I? Fine. You'll be better off when I'm gone . . .

(*He glares round the terrace, looking for a place to leave.* SOPHIA *and* SERGEI *stand by the garden steps.* PLATONOV *shakes his head crazily. Lunges for the terrace rail.* SASHENKA *runs forward again, grabs him round the waist, he swings round viciously, his elbow sends her flying to the floor, he vaults the rail into the garden, charges off into the dark. People crowd round the floored* SASHENKA, *who struggles to her feet screaming his name and takes off after him. A still moment, as people gather sombrely at the front rail of the terrace to chart their shouted progress. The voices slowly die.*)

ANNA: (*Finally*) Yasha!

(*Black.*)

SASHENKA's *voice, distant, slowly closing:* Misha, Misha, Mishenka . . .

Fade up:
Ghostly dawn light, moments before sunrise. PLATONOV *stands*
motionless, eyes closed, on the plank bridge on which the day began.
His wife's voice grows closer.

PLATONOV: Forgive me. Forgive me.
    (*He opens his eyes. The faintest tinge of pink touches his skin
    from the rising sun.*)
    Not another day. Not another day.
SASHENKA: (*Closer*) Misha. Mishenka.
    (*He climbs out, ready to leap. Black. Light up.* SASHENKA
    *appears on the bridge almost at once. A deep thudding splash
    below. She stares down in almost comical horror, fingers stuffed
    in her mouth. Rushes from the bridge. A slow salmony blush
    begins to colour the space. Silence. A figure slowly rises, down
    below:* PLATONOV, *drenched to the skin, fetlock-deep in shallow
    water. He stares hopelessly at the heavens.*)
PLATONOV: You make it hard, Lord. Really.
    (SASHENKA *rushes on, wades out to grab him to her. He stands in
    her arms like a rag doll as she speaks, water dripping from his
    panama hat.*)
SASHENKA: (*Part litany; all love*) Misha, my dearest man, my
    love, my husband. You live, then I live too. I love you so
    much. Misha, you're my world, air, food, roof, everything. I
    fear nothing now, nothing I cannot endure, no one will ever
    love you as I do. Sleep, Mishka, you must sleep, rest and
    we'll be happy again, so many fine days ahead of us, luck will
    smile on us, we'll see a bright new life, new friends to
    understand and forgive us. But you must learn to love,
    Misha. Love. So long as there's love, there's life too, long
    and happy . . .
    (*Sounds of the others arriving at the lakeside. She holds him out
    to look at him.*)
PLATONOV: Dear Sasha. Save me. Why is it always like this?
SASHENKA: Sh. Come.
    (*She leads him off. He stops. Stoops to rub his leg.*)
PLATONOV: Forgive me. I hurt my leg. I thought it was deep. It
    isn't . . .

(*She leads him off: he goes on whimpering, her child again. The rest of the household, in various stages of undress, stand in rough line to greet them.* YASHA *fusses up and down, with coats and capes and wraps. Greetings, hugs, kisses: another crisis over.*)

ANNA: Nothing will change, my friends.

(*The sun suddenly strengthens. They turn, like spectres, to watch it lift over the hill across the lake.*)

COLONEL: The sun.

TRILETSKI: The sun.

SOPHIA: (*Hand in* SERGEI's) Another day.

PLATONOV: Another day.

SERGEI: God bless us all.

PORFIRY: He will, he will.

TRILETSKI: Of course, I was a younger man then, and just a touch shy . . .

PETRIN: (*As if reading*) 'On the fifteenth of July, at the Black Forest spa of Badenweiler, his wife by his side, the playwright Anton Chekhov died smilingly. His last reported words were "It's a long time since I drank champagne . . ."'

YASHA: I love champagne.

SHCHERBUK: Aristocrat of wines.

ANNA: Nothing changes. Everything will be as it was.

RADISH: (*From above; unseen*) Grass dies. Iron rusts. Lies eat the soul . . .

(*The radiance spreads upwards; reveals* RADISH *and* ZAKHAR, PETYA *between them, holding their hands, on the plank bridge.*)
(*Looking down on the spectres below*) . . . Everything's possible.

(*Fade to black.*)